HANDS

The Complete Book of Palmistry

by Hachiro Asano

Japan Publications, Inc.

Published by JAPAN PUBLICATIONS, INC., Tokyo and New York

Distributors:

UNITED STATES: *Kodansha International/USA, Ltd., through Harper & Row, Publishers, Inc., 10 East 53rd Street, New York, New York 10022.* SOUTH AMERICA: *Harper & Row, Publishers, Inc., International Department.* CANADA: *Fitzhenry & Whiteside Ltd., 195 Allstate Parkway, Markham, Ontario, L3R 4T8.* MEXICO AND CENTRAL AMERICA: *HARLA S. A. de C. V., Apartado 30–546, Mexico 4, D. F.* BRITISH ISLES: *International Book Distributors Ltd., 66 Wood Lane End, Hemel Hempstead, Herts HP2 4RG.* EUROPEAN CONTINENT: *Fleetbooks, S. A., c/o Feffer and Simons (Nederland) B. V., Rijnkade 170, 1382 GT Weesp, The Netherlands.* AUSTRALIA AND NEW ZEALAND: *Bookwise International, 1 Jeanes Street, Beverley, South Australia 5007.* THE FAR EAST AND JAPAN: *Japan Publications Trading Co., Ltd., 1–2–1, Sarugaku-cho, Chiyoda-ku, Tokyo 101.*

First edition: December 1985

LCCC No. 84–082452
ISBN 0–87040–633–7

Printed in Japan

HANDS

Preface

The tremendous popularity of the occult that swept the world in the 1970s indicates how, as sophisticated and powerful as they are in this scientific age, machines and computers can neither satisfy human beings entirely nor allay their increasing physical and mental instability and suffering.

Certainly science has made tremendous progress. It is now possible to create aircraft with safety records of no more than one accident in twenty thousand flights. The traveler, however, is vitally interested, not in statistics of this kind, but in knowing whether that one accident is going to occur to the aircraft he is about to board. Science can offer no certain knowledge that it will not and thus, in spite of its great sophistication, in cases like this, aggravates instead of calming human anxiety.

In this age of automation and convenience, we can do many things without using our hands at all. One result of this convenience is a tendency to forget how wonderful the human hand is in the complexity of its functioning. Primitive peoples of twenty thousand years ago were more open in their wonder at the ability of the hand to make and move things, to perform delicate operations, and to express emotions with something like the expressiveness of language. Placing a hand on an ailing part of the body brings comfort and relief. More than any other organ, the hand sets human beings apart from the rest of the animal kingdom. The German philosopher Immanuel Kant was correct when he referred to the hand as an external brain.

This book deals with palmistry, some of the most ancient knowledge specialized around the hand, and seeks common points in palmistry as it has developed, differently, in the East and the West. Attempting to analyze a person's personality and fate on the basis of the hand is an ancient practice. It already has a history of more than two thousand years and will no doubt continue to play a part in the affairs of humanity for centuries to come. I shall be very happy if this book contributes even a little to furthering the study of palmistry or stimulates even one forward step in the further history of humanistic psychology in general.

In conclusion, I should like to express my gratitude to Iwao Yoshizaki, president of Japan Publications, Inc.; to the translator, Richard L. Gage; and to all the other people who cooperated in the production and publication of the book.

HACHIRO ASANO

Contents

2. PALMISTRY CLASSIFICATION 59

3. PRACTICAL PALM READING   111

1. Introduction to Palmistry

Brief History

Primitive People

No one knows for certain why primitive human beings, twenty thousand years ago, left the virtually numberless hand prints that can be seen on the walls of the Lascaux Caves, in France, which are famous for their murals dating from the same remote period. Some of these and the many other similar prehistoric hand prints found on cave walls in Africa and Spain resemble the prints kindergarten children with muddy hands might leave. Others look more like the hand prints made in the concrete in the entrance plaza at Graumann's Chinese Theater in Hollywood. Whereas some scholars consider them to be early attempts at human artistic self-expression, others believe they must have magical significance.

Because the hand prints occur in the innermost parts of caves, on the walls of which primitive men painted pictures of horses, cattle, bears, mammoths, and other animals that roamed Europe in their epoch, it has been suggested that these locations must have been places of prayer and magical ceremonies.

Since they were the main tools primitive people had to capture the animals they relied on for sustenance, the hands must have seemed not only mystical, but also symbolic of the entire human being. As Jack Mauduy says, if the hand print is taken to be the hand itself and, by an extension, the entire body, the spirit-strength within the hand can be thought to represent all of the energy stored in the entire being.

Religious customs associated with the hands still persist among primitive peoples today. The African Bushman cuts off a finger to symbolize suffering at the loss of a family member or loved one. Other peoples cut off a finger to use as a talisman against danger or plague. Plainsmen of New Guinea make hand prints on walls just as primitive man did twenty thousand years ago and cut off fingers to give to the gods in gratitude for good harvests.

It seems likely that, as time passed, primitive peoples stopped performing bodily mutilation of this kind and resorted to finding mystical qualities in hand prints, which came to replace severed digits and hands in their religious ceremonies. The same psychology may be traceable in an old Japanese custom of displaying on walls hand prints of sumo wrestlers as charms and good-luck signs.

With the further passage of time, human beings began producing hand-shaped talismans and charms. Muslims, for example, use such a charm that looks like a hand with the five fingers extended. In some parts of Arabia, people make good-luck signs over the entrances to their houses by dipping their hands in sheep's blood and pressing them against the wall.

In brief, since the dawn of civilization, human beings, not only in Europe, but also in Asia and Africa, have been fascinated by the mystical nature of the hands.

The ancient Indians and Carthaginians were the first to conceive of the idea of telling a human being's personality and fate from his hands. The Carthaginians left many stone markers dating from the fourth and fifth centuries B.C. and bearing carved hands; and Indian Yakshini idols dating from the third century B.C. often have hands carved in them.

Beginnings of Palmistry

From such evidence as three lines carved in the hands of idols dating from those times, it has been supposed that palmistry originated in India and the Middle East in about the second or first century B.C. Even when the palms are visible, there are no wrinkle lines in statues from comparable periods in Egypt or Greece. Indications of the lines on the palm do not occur in European painting and sculpture till comparatively late, at a time after contacts had been established with the culture of the Orient. The hands of statues of Christ and some saints preserved in a church on Sicily show such lines clearly.

The Bible contains many passages indicating interest in the hands; the very word is used upward of a thousand times. In Chapter 49, verse 16 of the Book of Isaiah God says, "Behold, I have graven thee on the palms of my hands; thy walls are continually before me."

And, in chapter 37, verse 7 of the Book of Job, "He sealeth up the hand of every man; that all men may know his work." "Sealeth up" means to put a seal or imprint on. In such a case, this passage seems to be a clear reference to the estimation of personality (or at least occupation) from the palm of the hand. In the Book of Proverbs it is said that it is possible to know the length of a person's life from his right hand and his wealth and glory from his left hand.

In ancient India, the art of *Samudrika* was used to judge personality and fate from a person's face, hands, and body in general. Kings are said to have employed it in choosing servants and in selecting the ideal wife. The classic called the *Ananga Lunga* contains a detailed account of such methods of discrimination, including *Samudrika*. Judging on the bases mainly of the hands was called *Hasta Samudrika Shastra* or *hastarika*, an art that dealt with the shapes of the hand and fingers and with the patterns formed by lines and wrinkles on the palms. No doubt, the designs seen on the palms and soles of Indian Buddhist statues are related to *hastarika*.

In general Buddhist sculpture and painting use positions of the hands to express spiritual and psychological meaning in the form of what are called mudras—hand positions of Buddhas, bodhisattvas, and divinities indicating attitudes or vows. There are six basic positions, each of which has a full Buddhist religio-philosophical explanation.

In the past the Japanese spy or scout called a *ninja* used hand positions to control mental condition. For instance, he was able to stimulate psychological unification by wrapping the fingers of the left hand around the index finger of the right hand. Interlocking the fingers of both hands and placing them on the abdomen was thought to have a calming effect.

Early Christian painting sometimes reveals various hand positions—the index

Fig. 1   Patterns of creases carved on the hand of a Buddhist statue

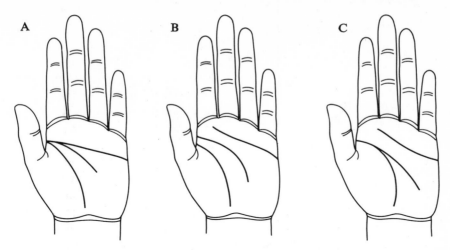

and middle fingers extended, the index finger only extended, the little finger and the thumb joined, and so on—that, like mudras, have special meanings.

The absence in their otherwise realistic sculpture of creases and lines indicates that the ancient Greeks were uninterested in palmistry. In contrast, in Indian and other oriental Buddhist sculpture, creases and lines are rendered clearly and in different ways to represent the characteristics of the particular Buddha: strong and vigorous for powerful masculine figures and gentle and romantic for feminine ones. The presence of lines and creases on the palms of such Buddhist statues is less widely recognized. In general, there are three patterns of creases, as shown in FIG. 1. The most common one is Pattern A, which is found on the hands of many Japanese Buddhist statues, including the colossal Vairocana Buddha of the temple Tōdai-ji, in Nara. According to ancient doctrines of palmistry, this pattern is the most noble possible to human beings and an attribute of kings. Using it on sculpture representing them means that Buddhas are the loftiest and most ideal form of humanity. In Japan, this palm pattern occurs in no more than seven out of every one hundred people and is often found in members of families of genius.

Palm pattern B is found in gently beautiful statues with a wonderful ability to appeal to the heart, like the figure of the bodhisattva Maitreya at the temple Kōryū-ji. Pattern C is found in such powerful statues as those of temple gate guardians figures called Nio in Japanese. In terms of personality, this pattern occurs in people who are active and fond of adventure.

I have already commented on the absence of these crease patterns in realistic ancient Grecian sculpture. The same absence is notable in most other Western sculpture and painting, with the exception of some early Christian art. And, when creases are represented in these early Christian works, the pattern is usually C.

Their occurrence in Buddhist art and absence elsewhere suggest that attempting to evaluate a person's personality and fate on the basis of the palm is related to Buddhism and probably originated in India of the first millennium B.C.

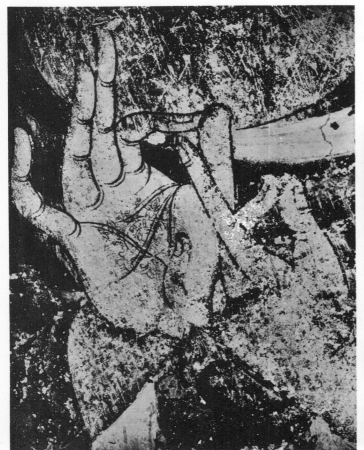

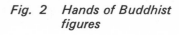

*Fig. 2   Hands of Buddhist
figures*

The hand of Amida as depicted in the mural on the
west wall of the Golden Hall of the temple Hōryū-ji,
in Nara.

The hand of the principle statue in the
Golden Hall of the temple Shinyakushi-
ji, in Nara.

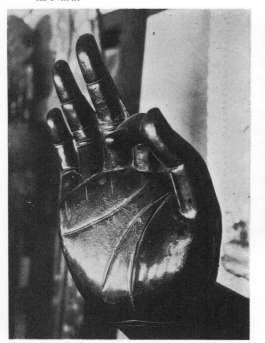

The hand of the principle statue in the Golden Hall of
the temple Yakushi-ji, in Nara.

Fig. 3 Oriental palmistry and physiognomy

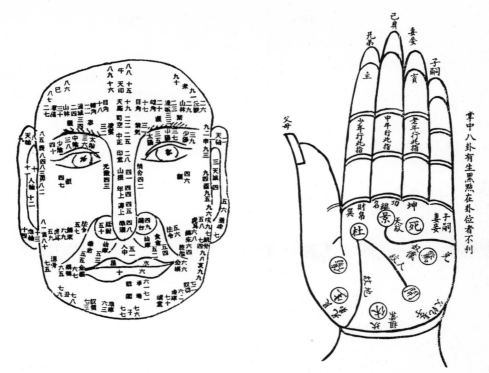

But oriental palmistry did not originate as an independent field. Instead it was an adjunct of physiognomy, or the science of judging a person on the basis of his facial features. The first written works about this field of multifaceted research appeared in China in 1122 B.C., during the Zhou dynasty.

Though not as old as this, palmistry in the West too has a venerable history. Aristotle, for instance, is said to have called attention to the physiognomy and palmistry of the Orient and Middle East as keys to understanding humanity.

But, in the West, palmistry has been known to fall on evil days. For instance, in the fifteenth century, together with all other kinds of fortune-telling, it was forbidden by the Roman Catholic Church; and all works on it were confiscated. Ironically, however, the first Western scholarly works on palmistry were to be published in Italy, the heartland of the Church of Rome.

The *Ciromantica* of Barthélémy Coclès and the *Introductiones Apoltelematicae* of Johann Indagine appeared in that country in the sixteenth century. Indeed, throughout the fifteenth and sixteenth centuries, in spite of the rigorous rules of the Church, human beings, true to their nature, had never lost interest in attempting to foretell their own fates. Research in palmistry continued; and with the invention of printing and the establishment of the Gutenberg press, books on the topic were printed and distributed, especially among the aristocratic class of Europe.

As in the Middle Ages people considered foretelling the future the best way to ensure continued existence in the difficulties of the present, so even today, in an age in which science is considered omnipotent, we are still enthusiastically attempting to unravel the mystery of our futures.

There are three methods of judging personality and fate on the basis of the hands. The first is *chirology*, which deals with the shape of the whole hand. The second is *chiromancy*, which is palmistry based on the creases and lines of the palms. And the last is *hand reading*, which analyzes the motions of the hand. From the distant past, the second has been the most widely used, though ideally all three ought to be combined.

As I have said, in the Orient, judging character and fate on the basis of the hands arose as an adjunct of physiognomy. Consequently, it tended to emphasize, not so much the creases of the palms, as the size of the hand in relation to the face, the form and fleshiness of the fingers, and the complexion and luster of the skin. This kind of hand analysis seems to have been popular among Japanese aristocrats of the Heian period (794–1185). For instance, in the *Tale of Genji*, one of the most famous works in Japanese literature, mention is made of it. In the chapter called "*Kiritsubo*," the hero Prince Genji mentions visiting, incognito, a famous fortune-teller (physiognomist) from Korea.

As is said in the parts of the Chinese chronicle called *The History of the Kingdom of Wei* (c. 297 of the Christian Era) relating the customs of Japan, the very ancient Japanese placed great importance on fortune-telling and included it prominently in national governmental practices. It was, however, generally performed in connection with natural phenomena and not with the human body specifically. For instance, it was common practice to put tortoise shell into a fire and then tell fortunes by examining the cracks the heat produced in it.

Later, however, telling fortunes and personality by means of palmistry and physiognomy were imported from China and Korea. And this is why Chinese and Korean physiognomists, who were closer to the font of knowledge, were considered superior to local ones.

In spite of the experiences of people like Prince Genji, however, it was a long time before Chinese- or Korean-style fortune-telling became widespread among the Japanese people in general. Though it is said that some Zen priests clandestinely resorted to a Song-dynasty classic called *Ma-yi-xiang-fa* (Easy guide to physiognomy), it was in the Edo period (1603–1867) that, with the emergence of an affluent merchant class, the people at large took a lively interest in the subject. In this age, many different kinds of fortune-telling achieved great popularity and became part of everyday life.

Mizuno Namboku, the father of modern Japanese palmistry and physiognomy, belongs to this age. He adapted the doctrines and teachings of continental practice and of the *Ma-yi-xiang-fa* to the needs of the Japanese people. It is said that he became a hair-dresser in order to have a chance to study the human face in greater detail, that he worked as a door keeper in a public bath to have a chance to make comparative studies of naked human bodies, and that he finally became the caretaker of a crematory to be able to study human bones. The original system that he worked out as a consequence of this study is called *Namboku Sōhō* (Namboku's physiognomy). In addition to this field, he devoted considerable energy to working out ways to improve one's future fortune and came to the ultimate conclusion that control of the diet is the way to ensure good characteristics in terms of both physiognomy and palmistry.

The important point to notice about Namboku and his evolution of a system of diet to alter and improve fortune is that it involves deliberate effort. In other words, throughout the Orient—not only in the case of Mizuno Namboku— study is directed toward first interpreting fate and then doing something about it. It is, in short, a kind of self-control system. In a similar way, whereas Western astrology reveals a possibly fearsome fate that human beings are powerless to alter, oriental geomancy—in some ways comparable to astrology—both reveals that fate and suggests ways to deal with it. It teaches that good and bad years come in cycles and indicates directions of action that will have either positive or negative effects.

Unlike its Western counterpart, Japanese palmistry—and physiognomy too— includes strong elements of deliverance. For instance, if a crease in the palm indicates misfortune, somewhere on the same palm will be found a line suggesting a means of succor.

Palmistry is the most popular of all fortune-telling techniques in Japan. (This is not true throughout the Orient. In Korea the system known as the Four Pillars of Destiny is preferred as is the *Yixue* system of divination according to the classic known as the *Book of Changes* in China.) Of the many fortune-tellers to be seen, usually at night, on street corners in busy parts of Japanese cities, the majority are palmists. The most popular of all is a woman who is to be found in front of a department store in the bustling Shinjuku district of Tokyo. The secret of her popularity and of palmistry in general in Japan is to be discerned in several factors. First is the simplicity and the sense of familiarity of being able to have one's fortune told on the basis of no more than one's own hand. But most important is the pervading of Japanese palmistry by the Namboku philosophy that, once fate is known, we must take steps to improve it in any way we can.

Importance of the Hands

The following are the major reasons why an examination of the hands reveals more about human condition and personality than that of such other part of the body as, for example, the feet, the navel, or the face.

1. Developed differently from the forelimbs of all other animals, hands are a characteristic feature of humanity.
2. The blood vessels, muscles, bones, and nerves of the hands are a complex

aggregation of elements revealing overall bodily condition.

3. A large part of the cerebral cortex, which controls movement and emotions, is responsible for governing the hands, which therefore symbolize psychological activity.

Now I should like to deal with each of these factors in more detail.

The Hand as a Characteristic of Humanity

The hands of the gibbon, chimpanzee, orangutan, and baboon have lines and creases and fingerprints but differ mainly from human hands in that the palm is crossed with many horizontal lines that do not alter on either the little-finger or

Fig. 4   Hands of human beings and of such primates as the lemur, baboon, gibborn, orangutan, and chimpanzee

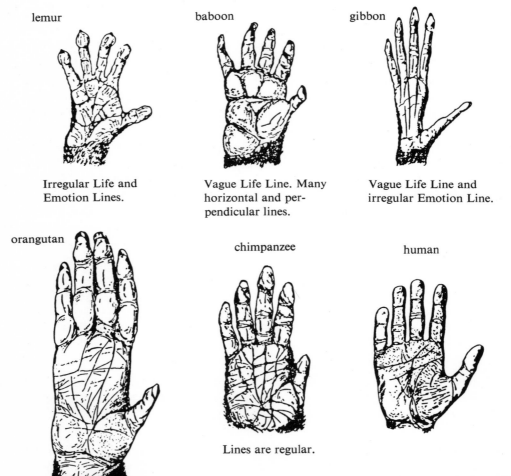

lemur

Irregular Life and
Emotion Lines.

baboon

Vague Life Line. Many
horizontal and per-
pendicular lines.

gibbon

Vague Life Line and
irregular Emotion Line.

orangutan

chimpanzee

Lines are regular.

human

Fig. 5 Comparison between the ways a human child and a chimpanzee grip a ball

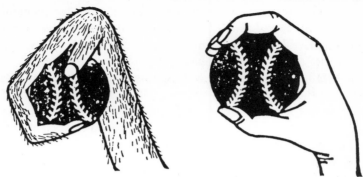

index-finger side (FIG. 4). In addition, ape hands lack the Intellect Line seen in human palms. What is the significance of the predominance of horizontal lines and shortage of diagonal and vertical lines in ape hands, which resemble baseball gloves?

In an attempt to answer this question, let us observe the operation of the hand of the chimpanzee, the ape considered closest in most respects to human beings. A chimpanzee grips a ball as shown in FIG. 5, holding it on the hand and resting it against the wrist. A human child, however, allows the ball to remain cradled against the palm and grips it with thumb and four fingers. The chimpanzee can move its thumb only parallel with the other four fingers and therefore must hold a ball as if pushing it upward with the thumb and fingers. The human thumb can oppose the other fingers, making possible pincerlike gripping. Because of well-developed muscles in the hypothenar eminence, human beings can grip things firmly with the palm. But, as any visitor to a zoo will probably have noticed, chimpanzees never hold things between only thumb and index and middle fingers but always use all four fingers, no matter how small the object they grip. They invariably move all five fingers together and never individually, one by one, as humans do.

The movements of the chimpanzee hand are very much like those of a human hand wearing a baseball glove. Consequently, it is no mere coincidence that the creases in such a glove resemble those on chimpanzee palms. Furthermore, examining the motions of human hands and fingers should provide a clue to why the palms are marked with particular kinds of creases and wrinkles.

For a few moments, examine your own hand. Put it palm down on a table and try raising each finger individually, beginning with the thumb and moving to the little finger. You will find that the thumb, index finger, and middle finger move readily but that it is difficult to move the ring finger without moving the little finger or to move the little finger without moving the ring finger. Turn your hand palm up and try bending each finger palmward. Once again, you will find that the thumb and index finger move easily but that it is hard to move middle, ring, and little fingers individually.

Most human beings know very little about the highly complex hand structure that makes moving thumb and index finger easiest and independent motion of the other three fingers more difficult. A comparison of x-ray photographs of human and ape hands provides enlightening information (FIG. 6). First, whereas in the human hand the index finger is considerably longer than the little finger, in the ape hand the two are approximately the same length. The human thumb is shorter than all the other fingers, but the differential between it and the others is much less than in the ape hand. Ape thumbs are very much shorter than the other fingers, though they are more highly developed in species that more closely approximate humanity in developmental stage.

M. F. A. Montagu* provides these statistics for length relationships between thumb and middle finger in human beings and apes.

The following are thumb lengths when middle-finger length is taken to be 100.

Orangutan	30.2	Gibbon	48.8
Baboon	35.2	Black man	56.0
Chimpanzee	35.4	Japanese and Chinese	57.2
Gorilla	37.4	Englishman	57.7

In terms of bone structure, whereas the human wrist consists of eight bones, there are nine in the ape wrist. In terms of muscles, the ape thumb is much less developed than the human one. The gibbon is the only ape to have a separate muscle for moving the thumb, and even this is weaker than the corresponding human muscle. In the chimpanzee and the orangutan, the thumb and index finger cannot be moved independent of each other since their muscles are connected, as are the flexor digitorum muscle, which flexes the fingers other than the thumb; the extensor digitorum communis muscle, which extends them; and the lumbrical muscle, which controls movement of the palm. All these muscles are different in human beings and apes.

In the human hand, though the muscles controlling the motion of the little, middle, and ring fingers are often connected, other muscles, especially those of the index and middle fingers, are often clearly differentiated. In a report submitted to the Fourth General Conference of the Japan Association of Hand Surgery, Doctors Matsui and Matsuzaki, of Kyushu University, said that only 16.6 percent of the people they examined were capable of moving their little fingers independently. In all other cases, when the little finger was moved, the ring and middle fingers moved too, indicating muscular connection among the three. The same report states that the lumbrical muscles of the middle, ring, and little fingers were connected. The index finger, however, functions with much greater independence. Only the chimpanzee and the gorilla demonstrate muscles for the hands compara-

---

* Montagu, M. F. A., "On the Primate Thumb," *American Journal of Physical Anthropology*, 15. pp. 291–314 (1931).

Fig. 6 Comparison of x-ray photographs of human and ape hands

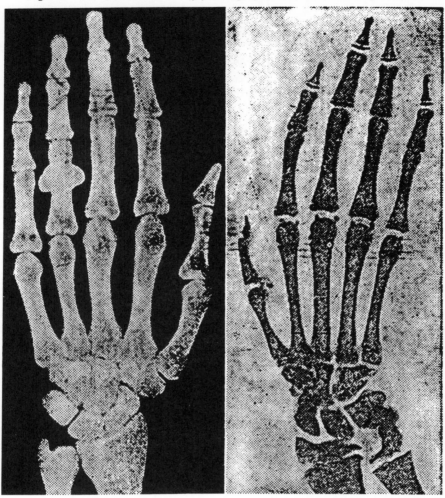

human   chimpanzee

ble to those in the human hand; but even in their cases, the degree of development is much lower.[1]

I have shown that human and ape hands differ in terms of bone and muscular structure, especially in the case of the thumb. What influence do these differences exert on manual motion? Ludwig Noire points out that the astounding perfection of the skill of the human hand depends on the possibility of opposing the thumb to each of the other four fingers.[2]

---

[1] Hartman, C. G., *Anatomy of the Rhesus Monkey.*
[2] Noire, Ludwig., *Das Werkzeug und seine Bedeutung für die Entwickelungsgeschichte*, 1880.

Undeniably, the thumb is of the greatest importance: without it we would be unable to hold or grip. This is why social-security compensation for serious wounds in the thumb is very high.

Though we tend to overlook it, the middle finger too is very important, especially in fine work. And the majority of our daily manual activity—holding a pen, dialing the telephone, turning the pages of a book—involves the thumb and index finger. (TABLE 1 shows the relative frequency with which each finger is used in typing.)

Table 1

Numbers of Times Each Finger Is Used in Typewriting the English Language

	Index finger	Middle finger	Ring finger	Little finger
right hand	1,490 (21.6%)	640 (7.2%)	996 (12.6%)	295 (1.3%)
left hand	1,535 (22.9%)	1,492 (18.4%)	658 (7.9%)	803 (8.2%)

From *Study of Motion and Time* by Ralph M. Burns.

Does it follow that, because we use our fingers—especially thumbs and index fingers—in ways different from the ways the apes use theirs, usage of the fingers results in the kinds of patterns in palm lines characteristic of human beings? If digital usage determines palm patterns, people who move their fingers a great deal, like typists and keypunchers, could be expected to have many complex lines and creases in their palms.

To see whether this is the case, I examined the palms of key punchers and typists working for a large Tokyo insurance firm and found a few cases in which lines were numerous or broken but no patterns seeming to have been determined by digital movement. In addition, the palms of a considerable number of woman college students who engaged in practically no manual labor of any kind were crisscrossed by many lines, sometimes with multiple examples of the three major ones: Life, Emotion, and Intellect.

At the outset of this comparative discussion of human and ape hands, I assumed the dissectionist's standpoint that digital movement determines palm pattern. Now, as a result of my examination of the hands of typists and key-punchers, it seems that digital movement alone is not the explanation. It therefore becomes necessary to seek some other factor accounting for the dissimilar characteristics of human and ape hands.

Research by such men as V. Horsley (apes) and W. Penfield (human beings) has shown that it is the motor area of the cerebral cortex located immediately in front of the fissure of Rolando in the cerebrum that controls the movement of the hands, as well as of the rest of the body. This motor area is divided according to the area of the body it controls, as is shown in the chart in (B) of FIG. 7. Stimulation of the part of the motor area of the cerebral cortex controlling the little finger causes reaction in the little finger. As the chart shows, the part of the motor area devoted

Fig. 7   Motor and sensorial areas of the cerebral cortex

The part of the cerebral cortex responsible for control of the hand is large and is subdivided by finger. (Chart by Penfield)

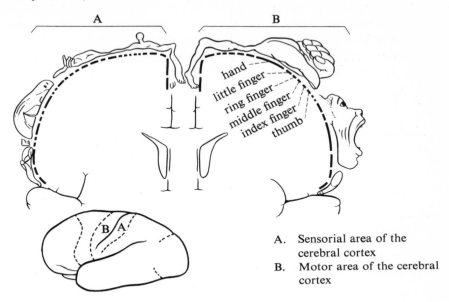

A. hand
little finger
ring finger
middle finger
index finger
thumb

B A

A. Sensorial area of the cerebral cortex
B. Motor area of the cerebral cortex

to control of the hands is very large, accounting for about one-third of the whole. As well as in the motor area, the role of the hands in the sensorial area, which orders and regulates motion, is great.

In apes, on the other hand, the motor area governing the hands is smaller than in human beings and is not subdivided by finger. It is conceivable therefore that the size and subdivision of the human motor area accounts.for the functional complexity of which the human hand is capable. It is unclear, however, whether this development of the cerebral cortex had already been achieved in primitive humanity or whether it has come about as the functioning of the hands has become more sophisticated. Anthropologists have argued this question for a long time, but recently the generally accepted view has come to be subdivision of the motor area as an outcome of increasing complexity in manual and digital operation as hominoids descended from the trees and challenged the variety of tasks their hands had to carry out if survival on the ground were to be possible. Because their life-style remained arboreal, chimpanzees and gorillas have reached a state of evolution different from that of humanity; and this shows in their hands. Coming down to the ground and standing upright greatly stimulated the evolutional development of the human hand.

As G. Révész said, liberating them from a locomotional role transformed hands into tools for other kinds of work.* This did not take place in the cases of such

* Révész, G., *La Fonction Sociologique de la Main Animal*, 1928.

primates as chimpanzees and gorillas, the hands of which have remained at a lower stage of development.

On the basis of the idea that the individual recapitulates entire species, I should now like to think in terms of embryology and developmental psychology in the hope of determining whether the evolution of the human hand accounts for the difference between the patterns of lines in its palm and those in the palms of the other primates.

In the human fetus, the upper limbs appear in about the first or second fetal month, though they are still undifferentiated into arms, hands, and fingers (FIG. 8). At this time, the protuberance that will develop into the upper limb is about one-

Fig. 8   Development of the bone structure of the human hand

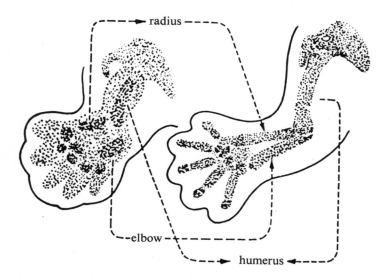

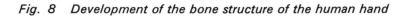

Fig. 9   Functional development of the hand in the human fetus

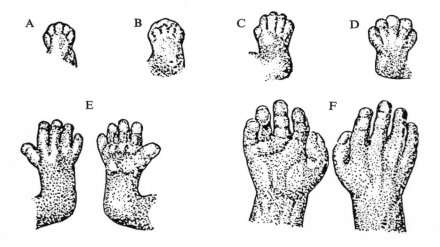

eighth the size of the entire fetus. It is important to note that the upper limbs take form before the lower ones. In the early stage (FIG. 9-A), the end of the appendage is marked with five creases. This terminal part develops rapidly and projects beyond the central trunk. In the second fetal month, the thumb develops rapidly to separate itself from the other four fingers. Gradually the bones take shape,* as do the other four fingers. In the seventh or eighth fetal month, nerves and muscles have developed; and the three major creases of the palm—especially the Life Line—have already appeared (FIG. 9-E).

In the postnatal stage, the hands continue to develop morphologically and functionally. Less than twenty minutes after birth, the infant, probably acting on instincts acquired in the womb, begins sucking its fingers and raising its arms toward its head. This raising of the hands is the motion the newborn infant performs most and is unconscious. Deliberateness of motion increases as vision improves.

In the series of photographs he took for his book *An Experimental Study of Prehension in Infants*, the American scholar H. M. Halverson shows how infants first see things that stimulate them, still without making motion, and then later stretch out their hands toward the stimulating object. FIG. 10 shows the ways infants move their hands and fingers to grip these objects. At first they can do no more than enclose the thing in the whole hand, palm and fingers. Later, however,

Fig. 10 Developmental stages in the way an infant uses the fingers in gripping objects

One month
Grips with entire hand.

Four months
Able to oppose the thumb
to the other fingers.

Seven months
Index and middle fingers
able to work together but
independent of other fingers.

Ten months
Index finger able to work
independent of all other
fingers; ring and little fingers
relax.

One year
Hand able to function in the
three basic ways.

* Arey, L., *Development Anatomy Pattern: Human Embryology*.

they oppose the thumb to the fingers, thus performing the first and most important work of the human hand.

The next major evolutionary development is the ability to move and use the index and middle fingers independently from the other fingers. This facilitates gripping, though the infant still lacks complete control of its hands and the objects it wishes to hold.

In the third stage, the middle finger, which heretofore has moved only together with the index finger, acquires the ability to move independently; and the little and ring fingers, which have remained in a state of tension, relax and gain freedom of motion.

These three functional extensions occur from the ages of one to five. Much research has been done on the subject, but child psychologist B. Hurlock has said* that ideally a child should be able to perform the following hand motions at the ages indicated.

At the age of one, to grip a pencil and remove a paper hat from its own head.

At the age of two, open a box, remove the cork from a bottle, turn the pages of a book, pile four or five blocks on each other, thrust a nail into soap.

At the age of three, to take basic care of the things around it, to dress and eat unassisted, and to pile up blocks as shown in a model.

At the age of four or five, to make triangles by folding a six-inch piece of paper in half, to draw by copying a quadrangular figure, to draw a recognizable human figure, and to use scissors.

As this study shows, at one, a child is capable of taking off a paper hat and gripping a pencil. This means that the thumb and index and middle fingers have developed to an extent. They have not yet advanced to the stage, however, where the child is able to remove a hat of a softer material or actually write or make marks with the pencil. To perform tasks of this kind requires differentiation among the motions of the thumb; the middle finger, which provides support; and the index finger, which determines direction. In a child of one year, the thumb moves independently; but, since the index and middle fingers can function only together, the hand is capable of holding only one object and the kind of object that has few projections. Between the ages of two and five, the hand develops to the stage where it can perform its basic functions; after the age of five, these functional abilities are perfected to the point where the child can color coloring books and make paper cutouts.

Between infancy and youth, still another important functional development occurs: that of the hypothenar, or the fleshy prominence at the base of the little finger, which in adulthood frequently plays an important part in manual manipulations. Though, in complex motions, supporting, and gripping, the fingers play the principle part, the thenar (fleshy prominence at the base of the thumb) and hypothenar are highly useful in large motions, rotating, changing directions, or steering to left or right and front or back. In work of this kind, the hypothenar is

---

* Hurlock, B., *Child Development.*

Fig. 11 *X-ray photographs of the hand and arm of a human male*

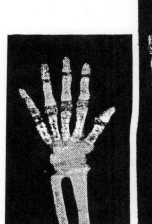
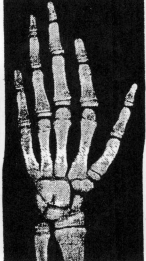
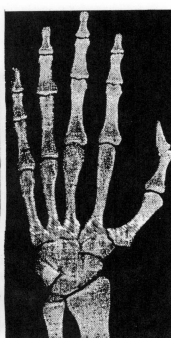

the center of power. It is the point of support in the quick motions of gripping the steering wheel of an automobile or handlebars of a bicycle. Furthermore, the hypothenar orders and regulates the functions of the thumb and fingers. Without its sound development, it would be impossible to write well. As should be clear from a comparison of the x-ray photographs* of an adult hand with the ones of an infant's hand (FIG. 11), development of the bone structure in these zones makes possible the functioning of the thenar and hypothenar in later life. Incidentally, such development does not occur in the hands of the other primates.

It is important to note here that, even before the hand and fingers move, the basic crease patterns of the palm are formed. In *The Principles of Anatomy as Seen in the Hand* (1943), F. Wood Jones says clearly distinguishable Emotion Lines, Life Lines, and Intellect Lines are formed in the palm of eighteen-week fetuses. An examination I made of a premature infant at the Department of Medicine of Nagoya University showed that the lines of the palm pattern are regular and orderly in a fetus of six or seven months. On the basis of charts in the work of the American embryologist C. Burton, the major lines of the palm form in the following order.

1.   Irregular lines form in the hand.

---

* Cole, Luella., *Psychology of Adolescence.*

2. The Life and Emotion Lines become clear.
3. The three basic lines are established, usually in this order: Life Line, Emotion Line, Intellect Line.

In summary, the three basic lines of the palm are formed while the infant is still in the womb and then develop further as the four basic functions of the hand are perfected with the passing of time. The evolution of the four-functional development of the fingers and hand is the basic source of the characteristic difference between the palm patterns of human beings and the other primates. The lines formed by the index and middle fingers differ essentially from those formed by the ring and little fingers and are not the simple linear patterns found in the palms of apes. Over thousands of years, the lines resulting from characteristic human digital motions generalized into the Life, Emotion, and Intellect Lines as we know them today. In chart form, the characterization of human manual functions and palm patterns may be expressed as shown in FIG. 12.

It is correct, then, to think that the patterns of lines in the human hand altered and assumed characteristic form as the hand itself became functionally specialized. Though, in an earlier phase of human development, finger movement altered, at the present stage, the pattern of these lines and creases has become more or less fixed; and such movement no longer produces new lines. The human palm pattern has been established independent of finger movement and manifests itself in the fetus. Just as, while recognizably human, noses and other features differ from

Fig. 12 Human evolution and transition in palm patterns

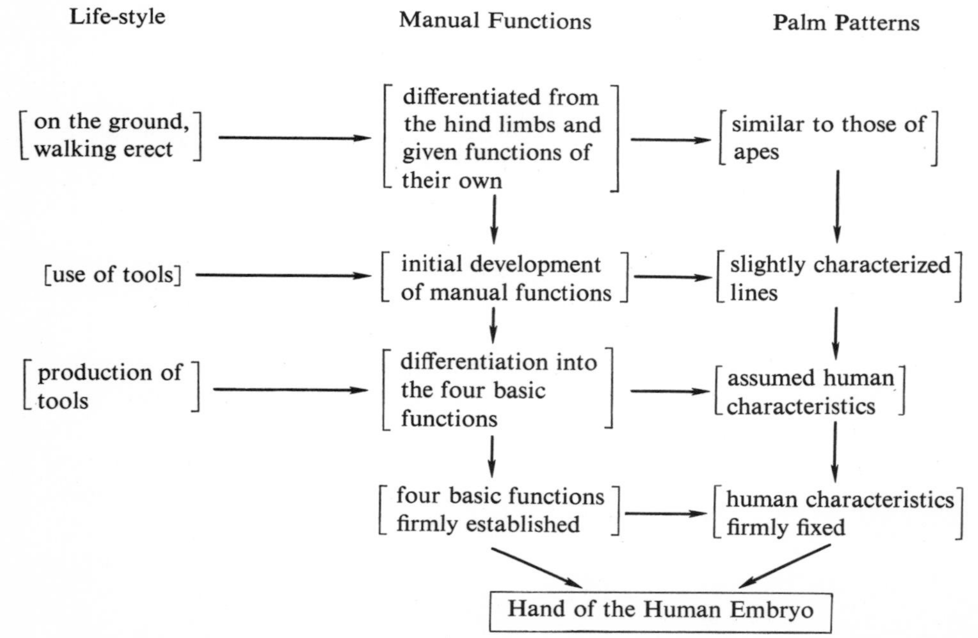

person to person, so within the standard human palm pattern individual differences occur.

In the fetus, the palm pattern evolves in the following way during the astounding development of the human hand. In the first and second fetal months, when life has just begun to bud, the five-rib-fan-shaped appendage that will grow into the hand has already appeared. In the two-month fetus, as shown in FIG. 13, the fingers begin to differentiate. The thumb (A) is especially well fleshed and grows more rapidly than the other fingers. The index and middle fingers, together, develop in direction (B); and the ring and little fingers, again together, develop in direction (C). As the hand develops in these three different ways, the fingers lengthen and differentiate. But, at this stage, the pattern of creases in the palm is vague.

Fig. 13   Hand development in the second fetal month

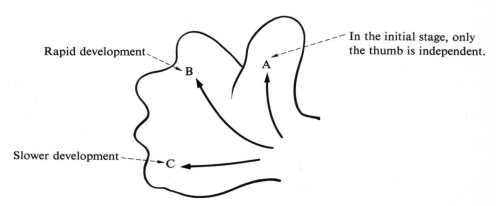

In the third fetal month, the hand can be opened; and wrinkles appear in the palm. As is seen in FIG. 14 (A), at this stage, the initially developing, fetal palm pattern is different from that of an infant. Only the line at the base of the thumb (a), which will become the Life Line, and the other line at the base of the middle finger (b), which will become the Emotion Line, have developed. All other lines remain unclear.

Fig. 14   Appearance of the pattern of lines in the palm in the third fetal month

A. Third fetal month   B. Fifth fetal month

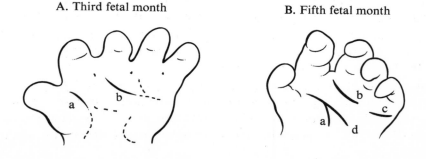

Research by the German psychologist B. Schulz has shown that, at this stage, there are individual differences in the size and fleshiness of fetal hands and that hand shape is being differentiated as a consequence of development of such internal organs as the brain and heart.

In the fourth fetal month, the line in the center of the palm that will become the Intellect Line appears. At this stage, the thumb alone frequently moves independent of the other fingers. F. Walker has shown that, at this period, stimulation to the palm causes the four fingers to curl inward. The thumb does not respond. The American child psychologist Arnold Gesell has corroborated this finding with different evidence. In short, at this stage of development, the thumb can move independently and develops independent of the other fingers.

In the fifth fetal month, the functions of the whole hand have developed completely; and, as is shown in FIG. 14 (B), line (c) at the base of the little finger has joined with line (b) to form the Emotion Line. With this and with the appearance of the Intellect Line (d), the three basic lines of the human palm pattern are complete. From the sixth fetal month to birth, together with the development of the rest of the body, the hand grows. As this happens, fine lines are added to the basic three in the palm pattern.

As this discussion has shown, the palm pattern of the fetus emerges, not all at once, but in a gradual and ordered way intimately related to the development of the other parts of the body.

The lines of the palm and even the segments of those lines are a record of fetal development. If that development proceeds normally, the lines will develop in dotted lines like those shown in FIG. 15 (A). Abnormality in development, however, causes breaks and poor alignment between the initial solid lines and the later dotted lines or in the center of the palm (FIG. 15-B). Broken Life or Intellect Lines indicate irregularity in the course of fetal development.

From the embryological standpoint, the palm pattern develops in three major zones: the thumb region, the region of the index and middle fingers, and the region of the ring and little fingers. The Life Line, which is related to the development of the thumb region, appears in the first and second fetal months and is therefore connected with the general condition of the fetus at the time. The Intellect Line, which is related to the development of the index and middle fingers, is deeply connected with the development of the hand from the third to the fourth fetal months. Analyzed more closely, the Intellect Line consists of two parts: the early one near the thumb and the later one near the little finger. The early one is related to development in the third fetal month, and the later one to development after the fourth fetal month. The part of the Emotion Line near the middle finger reveals fetal condition in the second month; and the part near the little finger, that of the fetus in about the fourth month.

Hormones and illnesses affecting the fetus in the second, third, and fourth months are frequently the causes of organic deformations. For instance, many women who took the drug thalidomide at this time in their pregnancies gave birth to deformed children. In many instances the deformations affected the hands,

Fig. 15 Palm patterns of normally and abnormally developing fetuses

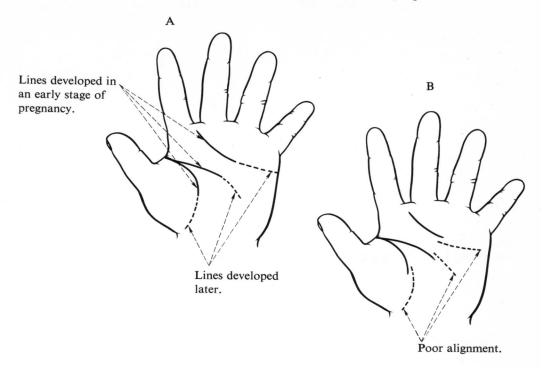

Lines developed in
an early stage of
pregnancy.

Lines developed
later.

Poor alignment.

which responded to external stimulus in this part of fetal growth by either developing abnormally or remaining underdeveloped.

The palm pattern of the newborn infant is a record not only of its own development, but also of its mothers physical and psychological condition in the early stages of pregnancy. (I shall deal with the relations between abnormalities and infant palm patterns in more detail later.)

It would appear that, since the palm pattern evolved gradually during the fetal period remains unaltered at birth, the fate that it represents would be fixed and unalterable by human effort. As a matter of fact, however, continuous observations show that children's palm patterns alter from day to day with astonishing speed. And, although at a much slower rate, they can be observed to alter even after bodily growth has ceased.

FIG. 16 (A) shows the palm pattern of a female infant of six months; FIG. 16 (B), the palm pattern of the same child six months later. There are so many fine lines in the later pattern that it might seem to be that of a completely different person. The vertical lines at the bases of the middle and ring fingers in the later pattern were absent entirely in the earlier one. Furthermore, the terminal wrinkles of the three basic lines—Life, Emotion, and Intellect—are very different in the two patterns.

Fig. 16   Comparison of palm patterns at six and twelve months after birth

A. Six months   B. Twelve months

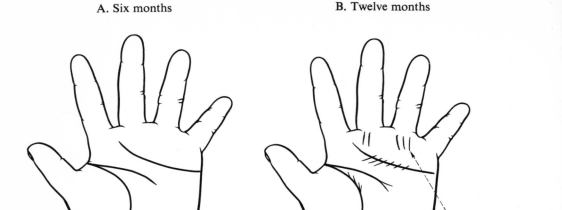

These lines have
increased.

Morphological Characteristics of the Hand —Four Zones

Functionally and anatomically, the hand may be divided into the following four zones (FIG. 17), each of which has its own characteristics. Number one is the zone of the thenar eminence. Including the thumb, this zone plays a role very different from that of the other three zones. The Life Line is located in it. The second zone comprises the little and ring fingers and plays a role very different from that of the zone of the thenar eminence. The Emotion Line is located in it. Since the Emotion Line stretches across the uppermost part of the palm and is called the superior transverse line; consequently, the zone is called the superior transverse zone. The third zone includes the middle and index fingers and their bases and extends to the central part of the palm. The Intellect Line extending diagonally across this zone is called the median transverse line; and the zone itself is referred to as the median transverse zone. The fourth and final zone, called in palmistry terminology the Mount of the Moon, is directly opposite the thumb and the thenar eminence. Degree of fleshiness of this region varies from person to person. It is usually fuller in men than in women and especially in wrestlers, sumo wrestlers, and other athletes. In other words, it is probably related to physical strength. Anatomically, the Mount of the Moon is called the hypothenar eminence, and the region the zone of the hypothenar eminence.

Fig. 17   Four zones of the hand

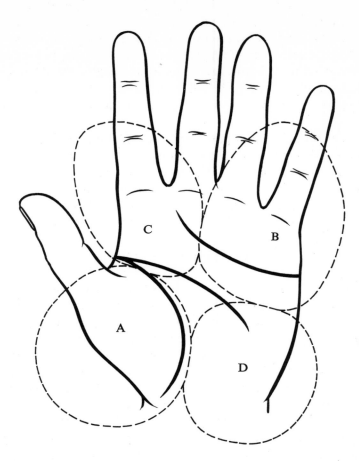

(A)   Zone of the Thenar Eminence

The ability to oppose the thumb to any of the other fingers is the characteristic accounting for the superiority of the human hand to the hands of other animals. It is because the thumb moves in a variety of complex and delicate ways in directions opposite to those of the movements of the other fingers that man has been able to invent and employ tools and as a consequence to create civilizations.

Embryology shows that the thumb is the earliest and fastest of the fingers to develop in the fetal stage (see FIG. 13). In small children, hand movements employing the thumb become numerous as self-awareness, ability to move and act, and intellectual abilities emerge. For this reason it is believed that the thumb is related to action, will, and self-awareness. And some research has indicated that people with large, long thumbs are active and intellectually superior. Length of the thumb is sometimes a racial characteristic. Irregularities during pregnancy and psychological disorders can cause deformation in the thumbs of infants. I have already shown how the internal organs and the brain develop in the fetus at the same time as the thumb. Because it is related to the part of the nervous system governing the area above the shoulders, from the standpoint of the oriental-medical doctrine of meridians, the thumb's functional connection with the upper body is very important. Stimulating the thumb causes stimulations in internal organs far removed from it and can be used therapeutically. Chinese medicine claims that the thumb exerts great influence on the entire body. In other words, the thenar eminence can be said to reflect stamina and the entire physical condition.

From ancient times Western palmistry has called the long line extending through this region the Life Line, no doubt because of the important role played by the region itself in the functioning of the hand. In the Orient, however, it was called the Line of Earth (*diwen* in Chinese and *chimon* in Japanese). In spite of the difference in nomenclature, however, both Eastern and Western palmistry agree that this line is the basis for judgments of the life-force of the individual.

(B) Zone of the Superior Transverse Line

The Emotion Line, or the superior transverse line, which connects little, ring, and middle fingers, is most apparent when the little and ring fingers are moved. In contrast to the region of the thenar eminence, where conscious motions predominate, unconscious actions are more numerous in the zone of the superior transverse line. The little and ring fingers are rarely moved independently and more often play a secondary role in touching and stroking things. Not only are they subconscious, but movements in this region are also less frequent than those of the thumb and index finger. In the alignment of typewriter keys, letters of low occurrence frequency are assigned to these fingers. Since their bones are slenderer and narrower and since they are less well muscled, the little and ring fingers are ill suited to independent motions. Nonetheless, these fingers are indispensable in many tasks. Without them it would be impossible to use scissors and difficult to manipulate a screwdriver. Writing would be irregular since these fingers control direction of motion in such activities. In contrast to the active functions of the thumb and index finger, the functioning of the little and ring fingers tends to be more static and to involve support, control, and fixing. In addition to such passive uses, the little finger is extremely helpful because of its intense sensitivity to size, breadth, softness, and hardness.

Since the distant past, the emotional connotation of the little finger has been recognized, especially in romantic matters. In French, happiness in love is said to manifest itself in an itching little finger; and what is meant by the English expression, "A little bird told me," is conveyed in French by "Mon petit doigt me l'a dit," or "My little finger told me." Twitching of the little finger in the presence of the beloved bears evidence to its emotional connections.

In addition, the little and ring fingers have a beautifying effect in such actions as holding a teacup or a cigarette. Buddhist statues often have gracefully arched little fingers.

Various congenital irregularities readily manifest themselves in very short little fingers or in abnormally long ones. For example, Down's syndrome, or Mongolism, produces short little fingers or sometimes little fingers with only one joint. Perhaps because of their locations at the extremities of the hand where there is greater possibility of damage during the developmental process, both the thumb and the little finger are susceptible to individual differences, deformations, and shortness. Charlotte Wolff has done research indicating that extremely long little fingers occur frequently in schizoid types. Abnormalities in the function of the little finger most clearly indicate irregularities in the endocrine system. Embryology indicates that the little finger is deeply related to the lower part of the body.

(C)   Zone of the Median Transverse Line

The median transverse line, or Intellect Line, is intimately related to the index and middle fingers and becomes most clearly apparent when these two fingers are moved. Since most of the movements of the hand involve the cooperative effort of the thumb and index and middle fingers, these digits are more highly developed in humankind than in the other primates and, in the human hand, larger than and functionally superior to the remaining two fingers. The largest of the carpal bones, the capitate and the scaphoid (or navicular) bones, are at the bases of the middle and index fingers (FIG. 18, c and d). Furthermore since the capitate bone and the lesser multangular bone (b) on the thumb and index- and middle-finger side are isolated and fixed in place, movement of the fingers themselves is easy. By contrast, the triquetral and hamate bones on the little-finger side (f and g) are mobile and unstable, making the motion of the fingers difficult.

Fig. 18   Bone structure of the hand

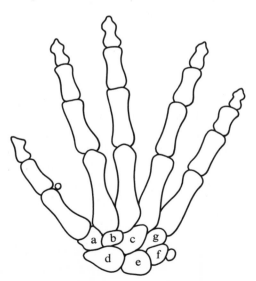

The Intellect Line (median transverse line) assumes a different form on the two sides of the hand: it is straight beneath the index and middle fingers but slants downward on the side of the ring and little fingers.

The index and middle fingers are strongly related to self-assertion and deliberate action. One points at something desired or indicates other people with these fingers. In paintings, Christ is often shown with outstretched index and middle fingers in a gesture suggesting a desire to be convincing or to explain something in a readily understood way. Pointing with the two fingers is a gentler kind of self-expression, whereas pointing with the index finger alone has a more forceful, even aggressive, connotation.

As I have explained, from immediately after birth into infancy, the movements of the fingers alter. During this phase, in which the fundamentals of the personality are being created, the basic movements of the hand too develop, according to H. M. Halverson, in ten stages. First, the newborn infant is able to do no more than stretch its hand toward the desired object without either touching or grasping it. In the next stage, the child can touch but still cannot grasp the object. Then he is able to cover the object with his hand. Then he becomes able to oppose his thumb to the other fingers and grip the object in what can be regarded as a primitive fashion but is still unable to manipulate it at will because of excessive tension in the little finger. Once the child learns to relax the little finger, the index and middle fingers are enabled to function independently. Finally he learns to tense the index and middle fingers only and to combine them with the thumb in pincer-like motions. The stages of functional development of an infant's hands may be summarized as follows.

- Enclosing objects with the entire hand.
- Enclosing objects with the four fingers without the thumb.
- Relaxing tension in the little and ring fingers.
- Tensing the index and middle fingers.
- Using the index and middle fingers in combination with the thumb to hold objects.

Development of the ability to use the hands skillfully has an immensely important influence on the development of the brain and the personality. One-third of the entire motor area of the cerebral cortex is devoted to the control of the hands. Of this area the region responsible for the motion of the thumbs is largest. It is followed in size by the area controlling the movements of the index and middle fingers. The area responsible for control of the little and ring fingers is small. The German philosopher Immanuel Kant (1724–1804) tersely expressed the important relation between the development of the two when he called the hands an externalized brain.

(D) Zone of the Hypothenar (or Mount of the Moon)

From ancient times referred to in palmistry terms as the Mount of the Moon, this region, which is farthest from the fingers and closest to the wrist, is less conspicuous than the other three but is also the region most clearly distinguishing the human hand from the hands of the apes in general. Its size and degree of fleshiness differ from individual to individual. Generally speaking it is larger and better developed in strong, stout people. In men it is usually broad (B type), well developed and fleshed, and virtually wrinkle-free, whereas in women it is long and narrow (A type) and wrinkled (FIG. 19). The differences are related to hormone secretions and to the development of the carpal bones.

Fig. 19   Forms of male and female hands

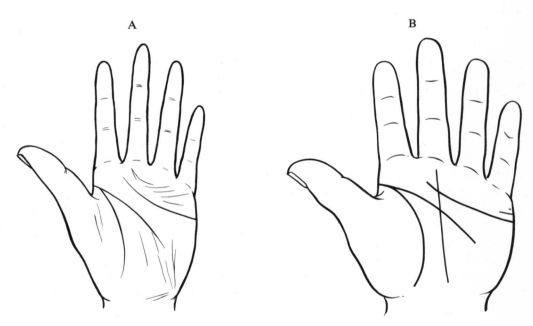

The distinction between infant and adult hands appears most clearly in the hypothenar zone. In infant hands lacking carpal bones, it is small and under-developed. In adult hands with developed carpal bones, however, it is much better fleshed.

Instead of being related to the fingers as the other three are, this zone is related to the carpal bones on the palm side. As FIG. 11 (p. 31) shows, the carpal bones develop in a peculiar way from immediately after birth to the age of twelve. They indicate the development of hormones, the state of the somatotrophic hormone, and bodily condition in general.

Although physiologically some people innately tend to manifest more wrinkles in this region than others, researchers like Charlotte Wolff have shown that the numbers of such wrinkles are related to the individual's personality and propensities. People who are active and have plenty of stamina tend to have a wider hypothenar zone relatively free of wrinkles. In creative and imaginative people, on the other hand, the zone tends to be long, narrow, and heavily wrinkled. Wolff says that in people whose powers of imagination and fancy are abnormal, this zone is abnormal and wrinkled. In people who are called upon to use their imaginations in creative work, like poets, musicians, illustrators, and so on, it is much more wrinkled than in people of a practical turn of mind or in athletes, military people, and people engaged in heavy physical labor. In addition, this zone is strongly related to sexual awareness. Western palmistry, in which it is called the Mount of the Moon, concentrates on its connection with imagination and creativity. In contrast, Eastern palmistry centers attention on its relation with sex. Incidentally, the left hypothenar zone tends to be more wrinkled than the right one.

The Fourfold Division of the Hand and Acupuncture and Moxa Therapy

In contrast to Charlotte Wolff, who thinks in terms of a two-part division of the hand, realizing that hands and fingers are strongly influenced by and extremely sensitive to changes in the mind, I divide the hand into four parts, each with its different functions and each responding to different mental operations. The physiological differences among the four parts of the hand are recognized, though as of yet their medico-scientific elucidation is incomplete.

Nonetheless, the therapeutic systems of acupuncture and moxa combustion, both of which have recently found wider acceptance in scientific circles, stress the importance of the hands in revealing, by means of what are called meridians, changes in internal organs. Six meridians concentrate in the hands in a way that clearly resembles my fourfold division (FIG. 20). Those meridians are as follows.

1. The Greater Yin Lung Meridian—in the thumb and thenar.
2. The Sunlight Yang Larger Intestine and Absolute Yin Pericardium Meridians—in the index and middle fingers.
3. The Lesser Yin Heart and Lesser Yang Triple Energizer Meridians—in the little and ring fingers.
4. And the Absolute Yin Pericardium and Lesser Yin Heart Meridians—in the wrist and hypothenar.

Recently, the meridian theory has been finding greater acceptance in the medical-science field since the meridians themselves resemble what is called Head's hypersensitive zone, where organic irregularities cause sensitivity or pain in the skin.

Fig. 20   Six meridians concentrating in the hands

Greater Yin Lung Meridian

Sunlight Yang Large Intestine
Meridian

Lesser Yin Heart Meridian

Large Yang Small Intestine
Meridian

Absolute Yin Pericardium
Meridian

Lesser Yang Triple Energizer
Meridian

Fig. 21 Dermatome

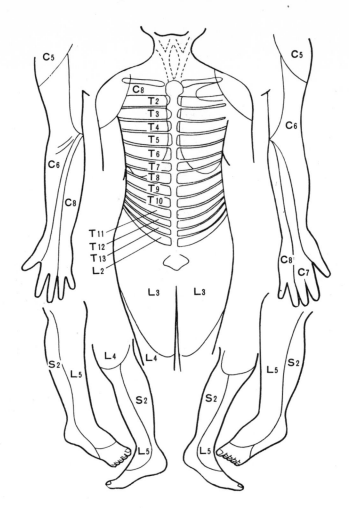

Among the numerous results of research into Head's zone has been the experimental recognition, as a consequence of study into the spinal cord dermatome, of parts of the hand that have very different characteristics. FIG. 21, which shows the hand dermatome, clearly reveals three different regions: thumb, index and middle fingers, and ring and little fingers. The concept that the four zones of the hand reveal directly the characteristics of the body leads to the following suppositions.

The Thumb Is Related to the Digestive and Respiratory Systems

The Greater Yin Lung Meridian covers the digestive and respiratory systems beginning with the stomach and proceeding to the large intestine, the lungs, the trachea, the larynx, and then to the thumb. In other words, the thumb is related to the digestive and respiratory organs. Numerous cases have shown that acupuncture and moxa combustion on this meridian actually bring about recovery in these organs. People whose thumbs function poorly may be expected to have weak respiratory and digestive systems, which are, of course, supremely important to both life and to psychological strength.

The Index and Middle Fingers Are Related to the Cerebrum

In acupuncture and moxa-therapy terms called the Sunlight Yang Large Intestine Meridian, this part is closely related to the head and chest. The meridian leading from the index finger passes along the outer side of the hand to the shoulder. The Absolute Yin Pericardium Meridian from the middle finger passes from the palmar side of the hand to the chest. In connection with the dermatome, this corresponds to C_7, which functions physiologically in the same way as the thumb zone. For this reason, the thumb and the index and middle fingers operate easily together. People in whom this functioning is weak may be expected to have weak respiratory and digestive organs. As has already been seen in the discussion of the evolution of the human hand, these two organs are closely connected with the functioning of the cerebrum. As the American psychologist Arnold Gesell has pointed out, infants begin to be able to use their index and middle fingers at about the fortieth postnatal month, or at the stage of development of the optic and auditory nerves and the consequent expansion of the realm of visual and aural experience. This seems to suggest that the functioning of these fingers is controlled histologically by the cerebrum. And this is explained by the connection between these fingers and the head and neck and by the way in which the composition of the nervous system is devised to enable these fingers to respond immediately to commands from the cerebrum.

The Little and Ring Fingers Are Related to the Heart

This corresponds to the acupuncture-moxa Lesser Yin Heart Meridian, or the Lesser Yang Triple Energizer Meridian, and is connected with the heart, the aorta, and the legs. As is seen in the dermatome figure (FIG 21), the spinal nerve ($C_8 \cdot T_1$) belongs to the nerves of the thorax. Professor Yoshio Nagahama of the School of Medicine of Chiba University has said that very shallow acupuncture on this meridian in patients with serious eye ailments produces a recognizable pulselike reaction, which continues to the heart. In *The Management of Pain*, Professor J. Bonica, head of the School of Medicine of Washington University, has said that the little and ring fingers are highly sensitive to alterations in the thorax and legs.

As anyone who has everly bathed an infant will have noticed, at the pleasant sensations the water produces, babies open and close their toes—especially their big toes—and at the same time, wiggle their fingers and outstretch their little fingers. Some adults as well experience intense pleasure from having someone massage the little-finger side of the palm and, at that time, tend to wiggle their toes. Similarly, when another person tickles the soles of their feet, adults often wiggle their hands— and especially their little fingers—in response.

The Wrist and Hypothenar Are Related to Nutritional Condition

This region, which corresponds to the Absolute Yin Pericardium Meridian or the Lesser Yin Heart Meridian and to the C_8 (cervical nerve) and T_1 (thoracic nerve) in the Western dermatome, reveals overall nutritional conditions because of the concentration of blood vessels in it. It is likely that the region is related to the endocrine system, which regulates the speed of bone development, since it and the pisiform bone supporting the wrist are very late developing, not reaching completion until about the time of puberty.

My Hypothesis

I believe that the lines in the palm of the hand relate certain things about the connection with these four regions of the hand and various physical and mental movements.

The Life Line
The muscles and nerves of the thumb and thenar, which produce the Life Line, are developed during the fetal period. The bones of this region, indeed, develop faster than any others in the hand. For this reason and owing to the connection between this region and the respiratory and digestive organs, the Life Line can be said to relate the conditions prevailing during the fetal period and the state of development of the body. When conditions in the womb were poor or when the fetus itself was weak, the Life Line will be broken and irregular. In other words, the line is clearly related to the state of fetal development and to general physical quality, although its connection with longevity is dubious.

The Intellect Line
The muscles and nerves of the middle and index fingers, which produce the Intellect Line, are the most sophisticated in the hand. Good, skillful use of the index and middle fingers together with the thumb requires considerable development of the intellect and of powers of vision. Using the muscles of this part of the hand demands a maximum of conscious control from the cerebrum. Consequently, with a little fantasizing and theorizing, it is possible to make some judgments about the tendencies of a person's talents from the Intellect Line, which does not, however, reveal intelligence or its lack, as was formerly claimed in much palmistry. I believe that the terminals of the Emotion Line and the form of the Life Line are more important in judging intellectual ability.

The Emotion Line

The muscles and nerves of the little-finger side of the hand, which produce this line, are capable of less complicated action than those of thumb side of the hand; and, developmentally, their control is deeply connected with the torso. Whereas the thumb and index finger are influenced by the somatic (animal) nerves, the little-finger side falls under the influence of the autonomic (vegetable) nerves and under that of the endocrine system. Since, for this reason, the Emotion Line is profoundally related to the internal organs (especially the heart) and to the functioning of the sex hormones, it reveals the individual's sexual inclinations and romantic and emotional tendencies.

The Fate Line

Not emerging until about nine years of age, parallel with development of the bone structure and musculature of the central parts of the palm, this line is deeply related to the functional growth of the hand and the body. Balance in the development of bones and muscles on the little-finger and thumb sides, with the bone structure of the middle finger as boundary, is responsible for the shape of the line. Loss of or irregularity in the Fate Line indicates imperfection in the functioning of the hand or even imbalance in overall physical condition. Instead of being a guideline for judging fate, as has long been supposed, this line is actually very important for what it relates about the body's state of physical development, emotional tension, anxiety, and attitudes toward life.

Other ancillary lines

The cause of the various lines occurring in the vicinities of the thenar and the hypothenar and the bases of the index, middle, ring, and little fingers is believed to be stress resulting in bodily disorder, changes in the endocrine system, and imbalance in the bone structure (especially the carpal bones of the wrist region) and in physical and mental state. Examination of irregularities in them provides clues for understanding physical disorders, psychological insecurity, and subconscious tensions.

Yin and Yang in the Hand

Yin and Yang at the Starting Points of the Life and Intellect Lines

In FIG. 22, the arrow marked (a) indicates the direction in which Yang energy operates. The arrow marked (b) indicates the direction in which Yin energy operates. When the two energies are in balance, the Life Line and Intellect Line will converge in the harmonious pattern shown in (A), in which Yang energy is strongest at the base of the index finger, and Yin energy at the base of the thumb. (In the following discussion of palm patterns, please refer to the various

Fig. 22

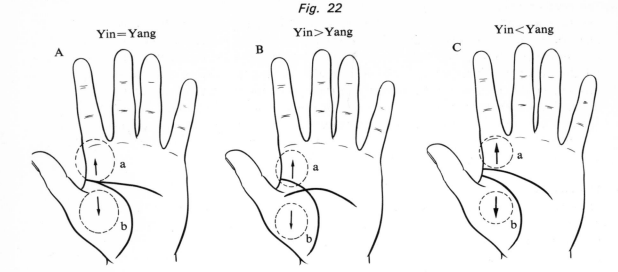

sections of Chapter 2 "Palmistry Classifications.") In Western palmistry, the base of the index finger is called the Mount of Jupiter, and that of the thumb the Mount of Venus. When the powers of these two mounts are balanced, the Life and Intellect Lines will have beautiful forms.

The personality of a person in whom Yin and Yang energies are harmonized will be gentle and tend to common sense. This is Type A.

When Yin energy is stronger in (a) and (b), the Intellect and Life Lines will approach each other in Type D. The personalities of people manifesting this pattern tend to be introverted and cautious because of the extra Yin energy.

If Yin energy (b) is still stronger, the balance breaks down further so that the Intellect Line crosses into or overlaps for a longer distance with the Life Line to produce the E-type hand, indicating intense introversion, reliance on others, and a negative approach. If Yang energy (a) is strong, the Intellect Line lies closer to the base of the index finger to form the B-type palm.

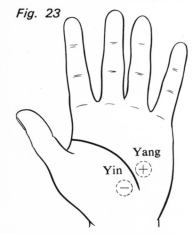

Fig. 23

Yin and Yang Energy in the Terminus of the Intellect Line

Though the balance of Yin and Yang energy at the beginning of the Life and Intellect Lines works variations in the palm pattern, the same balance in the terminals of the Intellect Line too play an important role (FIG. 23). Yang energy operates in the upper part of the Intellect Line; that is, the region near the little and ring fingers. Yin energy operates on the wrist side. If Yin energy is strong, the Intellect Line descends to form Type L, indicating a fanciful, negative, feminine personality. If Yang energy is strong, the Intellect

Line ascends on the little-finger side to form the H-type palm, indicating practicality, masculinity, and a penchant for theoretical thought. The O-Type palm is one in which perfect balance is maintained between Yin and Yang energies in the terminals of the Intellect Line.

Yin and Yang Energy in the Emotion Line

FIG. 24 shows palm Type I in which a gentle curve of the Emotion Line, located at the bases of the fingers, represents good balance between Yin and Yang energies. Yin energy operates in the direction of the middle and little fingers, and Yang energy in the direction of the base of the index finger. Strong Yin energy manifests itself in delicate emotional displays, changeability, and feminine reactions. Strong Yang energy takes the form of emotional control and feelings considered masculine in nature. Strengthening of Yin energy causes deformations and shortness in the Emotion Line in Type II. Manliness, emotional coolness, and leadership are shown by the III-Type palm, in which strong Yang energy attracts in the Yang direction.

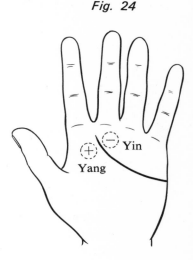

Fig. 24

Right and Left

Diversity of opinion about whether to concentrate on the right or left hand in palm reading has long reigned in both Eastern and Western palmistry. The oriental tendency to read the right hands of men and the left hands of women is related to the Yin and Yang philosophy of feminine and masculine (negative and positive) and to certain Buddhist practices.

In Esoteric Buddhism, which emphasizes the movements and conjoining of the hands, the right hand represents the World of the Buddha, and the left the World of Humanity. A person facing east has the south, the realm of the rising sun and of light, on his right side and the north, the realm of the setting sun and night, on his left.

In China, Korea, and Japan practically all Buddhist temples include somewhere a diagram (called *Taijitu*), which graphically expresses the oriental cosmology in terms of the forces of Yin and Yang. In this diagram, the Yin (female) element is on the left, and the Yang (male) element on the right. In contrast to the Western approach, in which a circle is bisected to form symmetrical halves, each of which can be colored white and black in a representation of the occidental faith in clear-cut distinctions as between yes and no with no interim area, the *Taijitu* is composed of two embracing commalike shapes (FIG. 25). The white (Yang) is on the upper right, and the black (Yin) on the lower left. Where one comma is larger

Fig. 25 Taijitu

the other one diminishes. But, even at places of maximum area, each comma has in its central zone a small circle of the color of the opposite comma.

The universe is believed to develop in a stable way when the forces of Yin and Yang are balanced; and the way in which the Yin (left) and Yang (right) forces harmonize has a great influence on harmony in the world of humanity and nature.

Recently much research has been devoted to the different functions of the right and left hemispheres of the human brain. It is known that the right hemisphere controls the left hand and the left hemisphere the right hand. The left hemisphere is related to theoretical and rational judgments, an understanding of numbers, and reasoned analysis, whereas the right hemisphere is related to powers of fancy, imagination, emotional activities, and aesthetic awareness.

Just as the brain is divided into two hemispheres, each with different functions, so the human face has distinctly different right and left sides. In other words, the face is by no means completely symmetrical. Placing a mirror perpendicular to the center of the nose so that it reflects only one side of the face at a time will result in a right and a left face that are so unlike each other that they might be the countenances of two separate people. In general, the right face has a cooler appearance than the left face, which tends to appear gentler. As some people are right- and others left-handed, so some tend to present the right and others the left sides of the faces when talking to others.

It is easier to demonstrate feelings and emotions with the left side of the face. This is why, at first encounter, many people turn the left sides of their faces toward the people to whom they are being introduced. Because it is simpler to manifest emotions and thereby create a good impression with that side, politicians and entertainers often prefer to be photographed from the left. Singers too, frequently try to create appeal by performing with the left sides of their faces turned to the audience.

In contrast to the left side, the right side tends to resist the production of impressions and to reveal the person and his feelings as they are. It is much more constant and slower to alter than the readily changing left side. In other words, whereas the left half of the face alters in response to environmental conditions, the right half could be called the basic face since it expresses the person's innate nature. The left reveals emotional reactions to sad and happy occurrences; the right reflects the person's condition with relative independence of emotion and daily-life circumstances.

Psychological differences manifest themselves differently in the right and left hands too. Some individuals consider the right hand central and others the left hand central; and there is a great deal of differences in awareness of the two hands. The difference in East and West as to whether precedence should be given in palmistry to left or right results from diverse racial ideas about the two sides and to fundamental philosophical differences in relation to humankind and the world. Some of this diversity is illustrated by writing systems. Whereas English and other modern European languages are written from left to right, Hebrew and the Arabic languages are written from right to left. When used in horizontal lines, Japanese was written right to left until World War II, when the left-to-right style was adopted, though not entirely: letters and manuscripts are still usually written right to left.

Right-left Differences in the Creases of the Palm

Long-duration observation of the palms of the same individual show that the creases multiply and change (FIG. 26) and that these alterations occur in left and right hands in different ways. Charlotte Wolff has reported that creases in the hypothenar region alter more in the left than in the right hand.

Fig. 26   The hand of the same man in childhood and adulthood

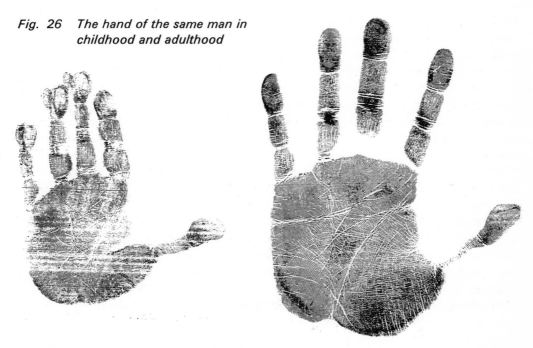

My own investigations have shown that right and left palm patterns are almost the same in 61.01 percent of cases examined and that the percentage tends to be slightly higher for females. The palm pattern called in traditional Japanese palmistry *masukake-gata* and considered the most unusual variation occurs in 4 percent of left male hands but only in 2.2 percent of right male hands. In 20.1 percent of all left hands examined, all three basic palm lines were distinct and clear; in right hands, this was true in 17 percent.

Perhaps the most interesting finding in my investigation had to do with the Emotion Line, which extends laterally across the palm at the bases of the middle and ring fingers. When the line was regular and smooth, it was that way in 58.8 percent of all right and 58.8 percent of all left hands. When it was broken and irregular, however, the irregularity occurred in 33.5 percent of left hands but only 28.5 percent of right hands. The most stable pattern occurred in 7.7 percent of all left and 12.7 percent of all right hands.

These findings clearly indicate that something—some psychological significance—is at work in the human right and left hands. It is therefore important to take the difference between left and right into account.

Which Hand?

Believing that the left hand manifests innate fate and the right the fate the individual creates for himself after birth, an Indian school of palmistry concentrates on the left hand for women, who are less active in society and therefore create less of their own destiny, and the right hand for men, who determine their own destiny to a greater extent. (Certainly, in many instances, inherited things are manifest in the left hand. Incidentally, the hands of people who come from noble families are usually slender.)

Much has been said about which hand should be given predominant consideration in palmistry. But the recent trend is to take both into consideration. Some people concentrate on the right hand and use the left for supplementary information. Some examine both and then concentrate on the one in which good and bad things are most clearly revealed.

Because of the controlling influence they have on the hands, it is important to take relations with the brain into consideration in determining which to stress in palmistry.

Gestures often reveal an individual's characteristics. For instance, when the hands are joined, with interlocked fingers, in a natural way, 70 percent of all people put the right thumb on top; and 30 percent put the left thumb on top. Until the age of about five or six, the way people join their hands varies. But, once a pattern has been set, changing it forcibly has an irritating effect. Many people who put the left thumb on top have vivid imaginations and dislike being forced into patterns. People who put the right thumb on top are adaptable and good at rational judgment. Often people who put the right thumb on top are governed largely by the left hemisphere of the brain; and those who put the left thumb on top are largely governed by the right hemisphere.

Close examination shows that there tend to be more and different creases on the hand that, when the two are joined, is on the bottom. In palmistry, it is wisest in terms of theory and psychological development to concentrate on this hand, in which the creases change readily.

Personality and the Shape of the Hand

Before humanity evolved more accurate ways, parts of the body were used as standards of measurement. It was convenient to think of lengths and areas in terms of the lengths of the fingers, the size of the clenched fist, and the distance from thumb to little finger of the spread hand. And there are close coordinations between the dimensions of the hand and those of other parts of the body. For instance, in general, the circumference (L) of the hand at the palm is one-third the circumference of the head. In an average Japanese this (L) value is 19.5 centimeters; and the circumference of the head is 3 times that or 58.5 centimeters.

In men, this (L) value is said to be connected with development of the testicles. In women it is related to the size of the pelvis. Since the fetus is thought to develop to a size corresponding to that of the pelvis, it is believed possible to estimate the size of the head of the infant a pregnant woman will bear from this (L) dimension.

The length of the hand is said to be equivalent to that between chin and hairline. Furthermore, body height is said to be 9.7 times the distance from the wrist to the tip of the middle finger. The circumference of the fist measured at the knuckles at the base of the fingers is said to be the same as the length of the foot. Since hands and feet develop in a balanced way, a person with small hands usually has small feet too.

Just as they are profoundly related to the size and shape of the rest of the body—a stout person has plump hands and a thin person has slender ones—so the hands have a close relation with personality, as Ernest Kretshmer was first to point out. According to Charlotte Wolff's study, the following things can be said about the ways in which personality differences reflect in the shape of the hands.

(1) Elementary Simple hand

Fig. 27   Elementary simple hand

The circumference of the hand at the palm is large for the body. The hand is well fleshed, has thick fingers, and tends to have a powerful, rounded-squarish appearance (FIG. 27). The prominences on the palm side are well developed and look bulky. People with these hands are blessed with good health and abundant stamina. This kind of hand is often seen on sportsmen or physical laborers whose work requires manual power. People with hands of this kind are optimistic and do not worry about petty matters. They are not afraid of hard work and have the perseverance to carry out even lowly tasks that others dislike. They work in silence and are inconspicuous. Nonetheless they are admired for reliability. In

Fig. 28   Elementary
          regressive hand

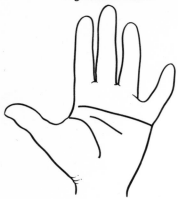

human relations, however, because they do not concern themselves with small matters, they are sometimes shunned for their lack of delicacy.

(2)   Elementary regressive hand
Like (1) a large hand, this type is however somewhat flatter and has a general squarish appearance (FIG. 28). The prominences on the palm side are less well developed. People with such hands have strong physical resistance and delight in work. They are prized and trusted because they willingly undertake mean tasks that others dislike. But they are clumsy at delicate expressions of emotions and are often criticized for lack of understanding.

Fig. 29   Motor fleshy
          hand

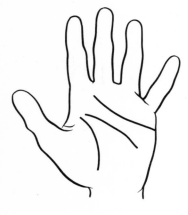

(3)   Motor fleshy hand
Soft and plump in general, this hand has long, tapering fingers that turn well back (FIG. 29). The prominences on the palm side are well developed, giving the hand a look of resilience.

People with such hands are sociable, imaginative, and blessed with good aesthetic taste. They are gentle, do not insist on their own way or opinion, and adapt well to others. In other words, they are easy to get along with. But they rarely give deep thought to life or goals. They tend to judge on the basis of sensation and frequently lead hedonistic lives. They are better suited to the arts or to diplomacy than to work requiring manual dexterity or perseverance.

Fig. 30   Motor bony hand

(4)   Motor bony hand
Palm and fingers are often long (FIG. 30). There appears to be practically no flesh on the hand at all. Because the knuckles are prominent, even when the hand is closed, spaces open among the fingers. The palm is very thinly fleshed, and the prominences on the palm side are undeveloped.

People with such hands are frequently strongly individualistic and persevering in their great desire for knowledge. Scholars and research workers have hands of this kind. Such people take more delight in the search for knowledge than in material or physical pleasures. They are stubborn and selfish. Though they have strong likes and dislikes in people, once they have made a friend they are totally faithful.

(5)   Small sensitive hand
This lovely, generally small hand with tapering fingers is
found frequently in women (FIG. 31). The skin is supple and
soft, the knuckles inconspicuous, and the overall impression
delicate. The palms of both men and women with hands of
this kind are crossed with many lines, indicating a high-strung,
nervous disposition. People with such hands are more strongly
attracted to art than others and ardently pursue ideals. Their
intuitions are keen, and their emotions strong. For this reason
they frequently demonstrate artistic talent and innate inspira-
tion. They know little of worldly matters and are inept at
making money. They tend to be frail and to lack stamina.
Consequently they are ill suited to physical labor. But, because of lack of perseverance, they find intellectual work too
difficult.

Fig. 31   Small sensitive
hand

(6)   Long sensitive hand
Similar in shape, this hand indicates a personality similar to
that of people with hands of type (5), though in this case the
character is more aristocratic and romantic (FIG. 32). Such
people find it difficult to tolerate severe conditions or poverty.
They tend to lose themselves entirely in love, and a comparatively large number of them make unhappy marriages that
often end in divorce. Introspective and easily hurt, they tend
to brood and be obsessed by ideas. Since tragedy sometimes
occurs because of this tendency, they require training in
thinking and viewing things in a bright, wide way. Furthermore they should take good care of their bodies since they
generally have weak respiratory organs and fall ill easily.

Fig. 32   Long sensitive
hand

Relation between Hand Shape and Palm Creases

In the history of palmistry, I have already commented on the two genres: *chiromancy*, which concentrates on the creases in the palm, and *chirology*, which concentrates on the shape of the hand. There is indeed an intimate relation between
hand shape and palmar creases. Charlotte Wolff, who has made comparative
investigations and reported on the connection between form and creases, divides
hand shapes into the following six patterns as mentioned above and says that the
paucity or abundance of wrinkles in the palm is related to the shape of the hand
and that the part of the palm in which wrinkles appear differs depending on hand
form.

1. *Elementary simple hand*
   (a) Few creases in general.
   (b) Horizontal creases more numerous than vertical ones.
   (c) Wrinkles deep and wide.
   (d) Severed or short lines apparent.
   (e) Attention should be paid to ancillary creases on the thenar and hypo-thenar.
   (f) Generally characterized by single, clear creases.

2. *Elementary regressive hand*
   (a) As is true in type (1), creases are few.
   (b) Horizontal creases predominate.
   (c) The creases are shallower and narrower than in the elementary simple hand.
   (d) More irregularities and broken lines than in the elementary simple hand.
   (e) Either highly localized or no ancillary creases.
   (f) The general composition is simple, though there are numerous severed and broken creases owing to the localization and number of ancillary creases. Such inherited irregularities as the F Type and the Inner Life Line (on the inside of and parallel to the Life Line), which I shall discuss later, occur often.

3. *Motor fleshy hand*
   (a) Though more numerous than in the elementary hand, creases are still few.
   (b) Horizontal creases predominate over vertical ones.
   (c) Though still deep and wide, the creases assume a clearer shape than in the elementary hand.
   (d) No defects and comparatively few broken creases.
   (e) Concentration of ancillary creases conspicuous on the thenar and hypothenar
   (f) Though more strongly characterized than the elementary hand, this kind is still frequently of the A Type, which I shall discuss later.

4. *Motor bony hand*
   (a) Numerous creases.
   (b) Vertical creases more numerous than horizontal ones.
   (c) Creases more delicate and shallower than in the motor fleshy hand.
   (d) Various irregularities conspicuous.
   (e) No limitation on the localization of ancillary creases of the kind occurring in the motor fleshy hand.
   (f) Line composition is generally complex but clear.

5. *Small sensitive hand*
   (a) Very large number of creases.
   (b) Creases run in all possible directions, though they often concentrate at the thenar and hypothenar.
   (c) Creases generally superficial and slender.
   (d) Various irregularities and severances conspicuous.

(e) General composition very complicated and less clear than in the preceding hand. Sometimes the creases are intermeshed in something resembling a spider web.

6. *Long sensitive hand*
   (a) Though numerous, creases are smaller in number than in the small sensitive hand.
   (b) All creases are intertangled and vertical.
   (c) Though delicate, the creases are less shallow than in the small sensitive hand.
   (d) All kinds of defects are conspicuous.
   (e) As was the case in the small sensitive hand, conspicuous ancillary creases occur in various parts of the palm, though they tend to concentrate in the Third Zone (the region linking the bases of the index and middle fingers and the center of the palm).
   (f) The overall composition is complicated but normally clear.

2. *Palmistry Classification*

Anyone knows the day and month of his own birth. To tell a fortune on the basis of astrology (the Western version or the Chinese version based on twelve zodiacal signs) it is enough to look up the right entry in the astrology columns appearing in periodicals. Numerology too is relatively simple. But telling personality, temperament, and fate on the basis of physiological exteriors, as is done in physiognomy and palmistry, demands specialized knowledge. This is why the other fortune-telling systems developed earlier and the more difficult sciences of physiognomy and palmistry at a comparatively later date.

On the basis of their different methodologies and theories, fortune-telling systems may be categorized as follows.

(1)   Fortune-telling on the basis of intuition or spiritual sense. This is foretelling the future by means of accidentally discovered meanings. Some of these methods employ tools like dice, playing cards, tarot cards, the bamboo sticks used in Chinese-style divination, crystal balls, and so on. Geomancy is an attempt to foretell the future by means of earth randomly thrown on the ground or lines drawn at random. Still other means of fortune-telling—for instance dream and spiritualist interpretation—require no physical tools but rely on the talents of spiritually gifted persons.

(2)   Fortune-telling on the basis of experience or theory with the aid of measurable rhythms of cycles. Astrology and numerology are examples of this kind of thing. In the West, the positions of the stars and their movements are the rhythms forming the basis of astrology. In Chinese astrology, however, not position but definite cycles are emphasized.

(3)   Fortune-telling on the basis of aspects. In physiognomy, it is the aspect of the whole body; and, in palmistry, the aspect of the hand. Divination on the basis of blood type is another example of this genre, as is the oriental system of judging things on the basis of the aspect (location and orientation) of a house (*kasō* in Japanese).

Universally, most fortune-telling falls into these three classifications and has developed in the order in which they are given here. Human beings first attempt to tell the future on the basis of fortuitously discovered meaning, as in geomancy; then turn to recognizable physical cycles, like those of the stars used in astrology; and finally evolve the more sophisticated study of aspects, as in physiognomy and palmistry (and in judging on the basis of gestures or blood type). Owing to the tremendous variety and complexity of human physiological types, judging personality and fate on the basis of the body or the palm requires both experience and knowledge.

Ernest Kretshmer and Willian Sheldon were probably the first scholars ever to categorize human physical types (three basic types) and to devote attention to the relations between physique and personality and disposition. Brilliantly completing work in this field that the Chinese and the Indians had long struggled with, the study of Kretshmer and Sheldon was eventually incorporated in physiognomy research by such people as the French psychologist Louis Corman and the Swiss psychologist Fred Weber, who, using a classification method similar to the one employed in analyzing physique types, scientifically studied relations between physiognomy and personality.

The situation with the classification of the hand is much more difficult. Charlotte Wolff, who has made psychological studies of the hand, employed a classification like Kretshmer's in many years of work attempting to explain the relation between hand shape and personality. But she encountered so many difficulties that ultimately she completely stopped research on the topic. When I met her in London, she flatly refused to discuss palmistry, saying that she had given it up entirely. In her late years, Wolff shifted from a scientific study of the hand to a mystical approach to palmistry, indicating a belief in things that the human mind cannot comprehend and that resist scientific explanation.

In my opinion, the Kretshmer classification method alone can neither explain relations with personality or disposition nor touch the most interesting aspects of the hand. In other words, in addition to the shape of the hand, it is essential to study the creases of the palm, which more clearly reveal mental and dispositional changes and physical characteristics.

In nineteenth-century Europe, fortune-telling on the basis of the hand was divided into one school laying stress on the shape of the whole hand (*chirology*), led by Stanislas D'Arpentigny (1798–1865), and another (*chiromancy*) concentrating on the creases of the palm and represented by Adolph Desbarrolles (1801–86).

Interestingly, the major course of Chinese fortune-telling based on the hand (called *Ma-yi-xiang-fa*) concentrates on the creases of the palm. And, as has already been mentioned, interest in these creases is reflected in the way the individual dispositions and natures of Buddhas are represented in statues of them by different patterns of palmar creases.

The following classification of these creases, which is similar in many respects to a German system, is of use in categorizing the lines and creases of the palm.

How the Categories Are Established

Examination of the two palm patterns (A) and (B) shown in FIG. 33 reveals three points on which they differ clearly.

1) Starting points of the Life and Intellect Lines (a). In (A) they overlap, whereas in (B) they are fairly widely separated.

2) Terminal point of the Intellect Line (b). In (A), the terminal point has descended well down on the palm; that is, in the direction of the wrist. In (B), however, this descent is considerably less.

3) Arc of the Emotion Line (c). In (A), the Emotion Line describes a gently curved arc in the direction of a location between the index and middle fingers. In (B), it moves straight in the direction of the base of the index finger.

Most hands can be categorized on the basis of these three major characteristics; but, as is discussed in the following pages, finer categorizations too are possible.

Fig. 33

A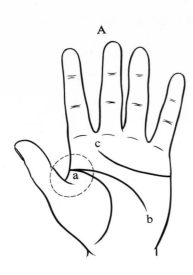
B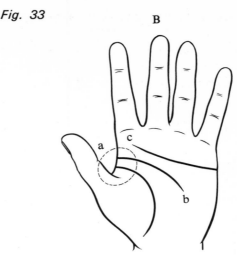

Starting Point of Life and Intellect Lines

On the basis of characteristics of the Life and Intellect Lines, palmar patterns
may be divided into the following six categories (FIG. 34). Before examining
a hand in this connection, it is necessary to draw a straight vertical line from the
point (a) on the middle-finger side of the base of the index finger to (a′) and to
examine the two lines to determine whether they overlap or are separate on the
outer (little-finger side) and inner side (thumb side) of that line.

A Type
The starting points of Life and Intellect Lines overlap, but the two separate before
reaching line (a)–(a′). This pattern is frequent in both East and West.

B Type
Separation of Life and Intellect Lines occurs still farther inward of line (a)–(a′).
Indeed the starting points of the two are separate. In other words, they come into
contact at no point. According to anthropological reports, the B-Type hand occurs
with slightly greater frequency in females than in males and is more common in
occidental than oriental peoples.

C Type
Though the pattern is similar to the B Type, in the C Type, the Intellect Line
begins on the outer side of line (a)–(a′) and nowhere comes into contact with the
Life Line. This pattern is infrequently encountered.

D Type
This pattern is similar to the A Type, though the overlapping of the Life and

Fig. 34   Classifications of types of starting regions of the Life and Intellect Lines

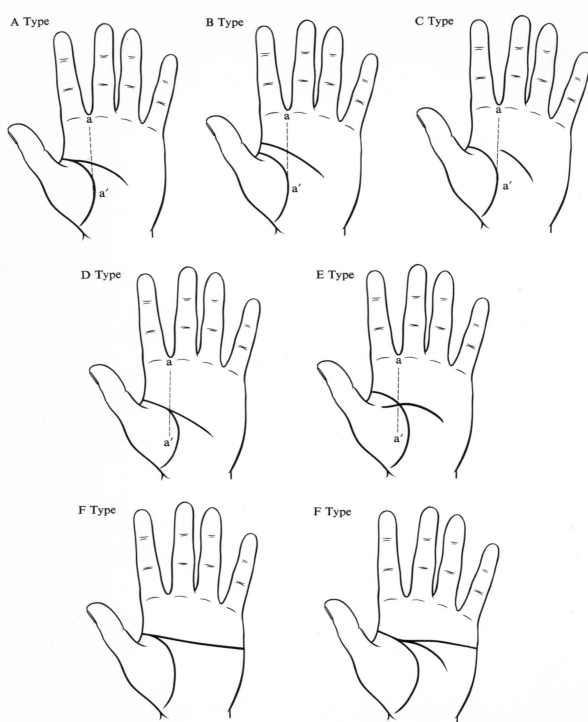

Intellect Lines is long, continuing into the outer side of line (a)–(a′). This pattern is frequent among Japanese.

E Type
In this pattern, the starting point of the Intellect Line is on the inner side of the Life Line, obscuring the relation of their initial positions.

F Type
This pattern, in which the Intellect Line is a straight line from the starting point across the palm, is sometimes called the monkey hand because of its resemblance to the prevailing pattern in simian palms. In anthropological terms, however, it is referred to as the four-finger-line pattern since it is most clearly apparent when the four fingers—index, middle, ring, and little—are bent simultaneously. Anthropologists say that the pattern is rare among occidental and more common among oriental peoples. In addition to the perfect F Type, in which one clear line crosses the palm, a modified F Type exists. In it, three lines converge at one point; and the Intellect and Emotion Lines cross the palm, giving the appearance of a single line. The F Type is frequently used in sculpture and paintings of Buddhas and other lofty individuals.

German anthropologists employ these categorizations on the basis of the Life and Intellect Lines in their research.

Classification by Orientation of the Intellect Line

In order to determine classification on the basis of this characteristic, first establish a vertical line (a)–(a′) running from the starting point of the Emotion Line to the wrist (FIG. 35). At exactly the midway point of this line, establish a horizontal

Fig. 35   Types of terminal regions of the Intellect Line

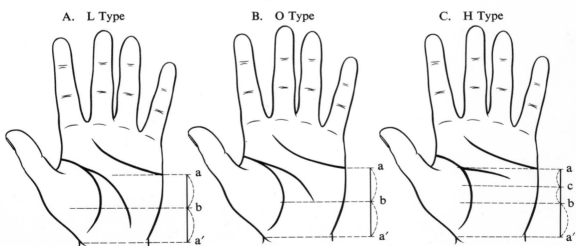

A. L Type   B. O Type   C. H Type

line (b). In A-Type hands, the Intellect Line will extend below line (b); in B-Type hands, it will stop precisely at line (b). Establish line (c) exactly halfway between lines (a) and (b). In the C-Type hand, the Intellect Line will stop above the level of line (c).

Hands in which the Intellect Line descends below line (b) are classified as Type L. Those in which it stops between lines (b) and (c) are classified as Type O; and those in which it stops above line (c) are classified as Type H. If the Intellect Line is doubled or branched, the clearest and longest line is used as a classification standard. O is the commonest of the three patterns. Occupation and life-style vary the characteristics of these patterns.

Classification by the Shape of the Emotion Line

The Emotion Line manifests alterations in physical condition so vividly that Indian palmistry refers to it as the Life Line. Consequently, it assumes many forms. Generally it is simpler and clearer in men and more complex in women. It is

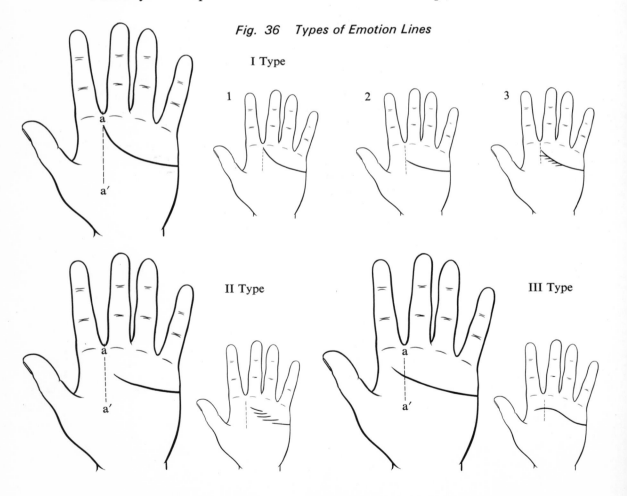

Fig. 36   Types of Emotion Lines

simple in hands that have broad palms and short fingers and more varied and complicated in hands with small palms and long, slender fingers. Classification on the basis of the Emotion Line depends on whether it reaches precisely, stops short of, or crosses line (a)–(a′), the vertical line drawn between the index and middle fingers and used in connection with the form of the Life and Intellect Lines (FIG. 36). In Type I, it stops immediately at line (a)–(a′). This type is subdivided into three subtypes: (1) in which the line describes a gentle curve oriented toward a place between the index and ring fingers; (2) in which the line does not curve but stops exactly at line (a)–(a′); and (3) in which the termination of the line is multibranched.

In Type-II hands, the Emotion Line either stops short of line (a)–(a′) (sometimes as far short as the base of the middle finger) or is broken. In Type-III hands, the Emotion Line crosses line (a)–(a′) in the direction of the base of the index finger.

Even the most complicated Emotion Lines can be categorized on the basis of these criteria. Of the three types, I is most common, II is more frequent in women, and III is more frequent in men.

Annotation

For convenience, hand patterns are given overall code annotations that reveal the classification according to relations between Life and Intellect Lines, the form of the Intellect Line, and the length of the Emotion Line. For instance, a hand in which the starting points of Life and Intellect Lines are separate is Type B. If, in that same hand, the Intellect Line is curved down, it is classified as L. And, if the Emotion Line is broken, it is called II. The total code annotation of such a hand would be Type BL II (FIG. 37). The relation between Life and Intellect Lines is

Fig. 37 Example of classification

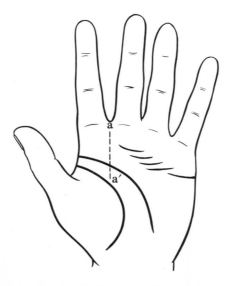

always put first and is followed by the form of the Intellect and Emotion Lines in that order. Once a hand has been examined, classified, and assigned such a code designation, it is possible to visualize it without the help of a drawing. This codification greatly facilitates surveying, scientific classification, and statistical treatment.

Palm Types A, D, and E

These three types, in which the starting points of Life and Intellect Lines overlap, are the most general in both the East and the West. As is seen in TABLE 2, the anthropologist H. Schiller has shown that, in various groups, 78.6 percent of the people examined had either A- or D-Type palm patterns in both hands. Different patterns in left and right hands occurred in 11.8 percent. The starting points of the two lines tend to overlap more frequently in men than in women. Although children both of whose parents have A or D palms are likely to manifest the same patterns, if either parent had B or C Types, the likelihood is great that the children will too. Further, if one parent has F-Type palms, the likelihood that the children will have either A or D drops sharply. From this information, it is apparent that, though the types in which the starting points of the Life and Intellect Lines overlap are standard and most frequent, the introduction of genes for the more distinctive patterns (F or B) easily causes variations in them. In short, these patterns are unstable and readily modified, with consequent corresponding alterations in personality type and physique.

Investigations of the hands of Japanese people produced the following data on A-, D-, and E-Type palm patterns, which, incidentally, occur with high frequency among the hand patterns left in murals created by primitive people (TABLE 2).

Table 2

		Type A	Type D	Type E
right hand	men	16.9%	58.6%	0.47%
	women	20.1%	52.4%	0.20%
	average	18.2%	56.2%	0.36%
left hand	men	20.3%	57.6%	0.35%
	women	22.7%	48.5%	0.38%
	average	21.2%	54.1%	0.36%

In contrast to the Japanese, in whom Type D, with a long overlap between Life and Intellect Lines, is especially frequent, in Westerners, Type A is slightly more common, and Type D rare. Type A in which the lines are distinctly drawn predominates in oriental Buddhist statues. Type A is more common in the left than in the right hand. TABLE 3 shows the relative frequencies of Types A and D and Type B, in which the starting points of Life and Intellect Lines are separate.

Table 3

| right hand | Type A | Type B | Type D | Type B |
left hand	Type B	Type A	Type B	Type D
men	20.0%	11.5%	18.6%	3.7%
women	16.5%	14.5%	16.5%	6.9%
average	17.9%	12.3%	17.6%	4.8%

These data show that, when the right hand is of Type B, the likelihood that Type D will appear drops and that little influence is exerted when the left hand is Type B. In Japanese, when the unusual Type F appears in right and left hands, the following percentages emerge:

Table 4

| right hand | Type A | Type F | Type D | Type F |
left hand	Type F	Type A	Type F	Type D
men	14.4%	1.2%	52.9%	1.0%
women	11.1%	0	33.3%	1.9%
average	13.9%	0.6%	48.8%	1.5%

In this instance too, when the right hand is Type F, the likelihood that the left hand will be Type A or Type D drops dramatically. Investigations by the anthropologist F. W. Miller have shown that cases in which the palm patterns of the hands differ are fairly rare and that Types A and D are more frequent in men than in women.

Types B and C

Frequency of appearance of these two types, in which the starting points of the Life and Intellect Lines are separate, varies according to race. Whereas they occur in only two out of every ten Japanese, they are more frequent in Westerners. The following chart is a sampling of manifestation frequencies in parts of Japan and regions of the world.

Ainu	15.6%
Koreans	4.0%
Europeans	14.3%

The Island of Kyushu	7.2%
The Kansai District (Western Japan, especially the Osaka-Kyoto-Kobe region)	13.0%
Eastern Japan	16.6%

As these data reveal, Types B and C are rarer in oriental than in occidental peoples and are more frequent in the eastern than in the western districts of Japan. Interestingly, it is common for women with B or C patterns in both hands to be the oldest daughters of the family. In Buddhist sculpture, Types B and C occur in powerful figures with somewhat frightening faces, like the Nio guardians of Buddhist temple gates, or in figures that are supposed to produce a foreign appearance. According to a survey conducted by Dr. Tokura Takao of the Tokyo Women's Medical University, Types B and C occur slightly more frequently in women than in men (*Journal of the Tokyo Women's Medical University*, Vol. 36, No. 12).

The same university conducted a survey on the occurrence frequencies of these two patterns and congenital heart malformation, using 300 normal people and 300 people with abnormal hearts.

Table 5

	Normal subjects	Heart cases
male	11.3%	19.1%
female	14.7%	21.7%

The following are percentages of examined cases in which one hand only, either right or left, was of Type B or Type C.

Table 6

	Male		Female	
	normal	abnormal heart	normal	abnormal heart
right only B or C	1.3%	5.7%	1.3%	4.9%
left only B or C	1.3%	7.0%	2.0%	3.5%
both hands B or C	8.7%	6.4%	10.7%	12.1%

In normal subjects, cases in which both hands were Types B or C were more numerous. Out of 300 subjects, only 5 (1.7 percent) demonstrated one of these patterns in one hand only. In subjects with heart abnormalities, however, the percentage showing one of these types in only one hand tripled to 5.3 percent.

Type F

Considered the ideal and symbolizing great nobility, this palm type (called the *masukake* type in Japanese) is associated with a powerful, commanding personality and is often used in sculptural representations of Buddhas. Anthropologically it is more common in oriental than in occidental peoples.

Japanese	6.0%
Ainu	2.2%
Chinese	13.0%
Swiss	1.2%
Dutch	1.5%
Gypsies	14.3%
Koreans	11.2%

Since, on the basis of the occurrence frequency of this hand pattern, it is possible to estimate the racial associations of a people, it would seem that such data could be a useful clue in attempting to solve the riddle of the much disputed origin of the Japanese.

In Japan, distribution of this palm pattern is greater in the western than in the eastern part of the country: 9.2 percent for Kyushu as compared with 4.0 percent for eastern Japan.

The English scholar Wood Jones (*Principles of Anatomy as Seen in the Hand*, 1920), who discovered the similarity between this pattern in human hands and the prevailing pattern in simian palms, named it the Simian Line.

People with this type hand are strongly individualistic and emotionally irregular. Though they may become very angry, they do not give the feeling surface expression. Their appearance and their true emotional state are often very different. Though apparently having a sense of humor and caring for the feelings and needs of others, underneath, they are frequently very chilly people. Socially they tend to be among the elite and capture general attention because of their excellent performance as early as primary school. In Japan, among leaders in all fields are many people with this hand pattern, as there were among the great generals of the Period of Warring States (1467–1568), one of the most violent transitional times in Japanese history.

Though frequently found in persons of genius, Type F occurs often among children who, for one reason or another, are difficult to deal with: for instance, among the mentally retarded or among children with organic abnormalities. The hand print in FIG. 38 manifests this type and is that of a victim of Down's syndrome (Mongolism). It should be noted that the thumb is poorly fleshed and that the little finger is short.

People with this type of hand tend to succeed in occupations requiring manual dexterity—surgery, engineering, architecture, shiatsu—and in such other fields as

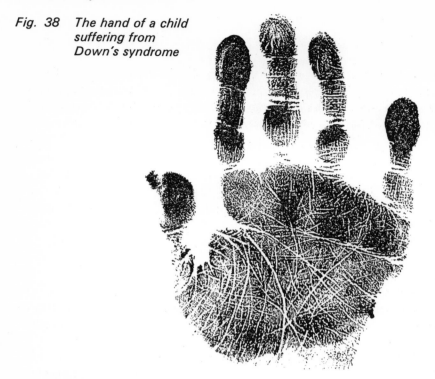

Fig. 38   The hand of a child suffering from Down's syndrome

television entertainment, work demanding original ideas, big business, music, writing, and so on.

Type F may be subdivided into (1) the Perfect F; (2) the Imperfect F; and (3) Complicated F, which resembles (2) F (FIG. 39).

Fig. 39   Variations of the F Type

A.   Perfect F Type   B.   Imperfect F Type   C.   Complicated F Type

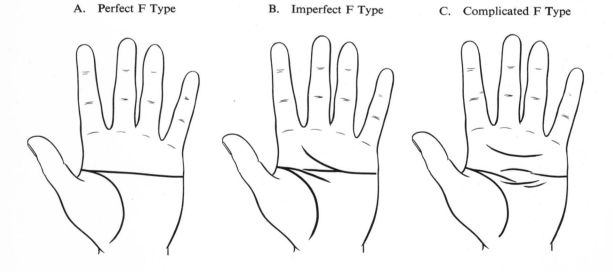

(1) Perfect F Type

A single strong and clear line cuts across the palm horizontally. Fine creases are few. Easily transmitted hereditarily, if both parents manifest it, this pattern will certainly emerge in the children. Type (1) F, the most commonly encountered of the F hands, is often seen in technicians; doctors (especially surgeons, radiologists, and dentists); engineers, and scholars. People with it frequently have IQs of above 130 and usually have good powers of judgment and analytical thought. On the surface rather ordinary, people with this type are generally popular and well liked and are more valorous and brave than might be foreseen. Though they seem aloof, they are actually considerate and kind. Giving their all to any kind of work they undertake, they usually play leading roles.

But people with the Perfect F hand find it so difficult to meet marriage partners that men with it usually do not wed until their thirties and women in their late twenties. They are ideally suited to driving automobiles or any work requiring skill with machinery.

(2) Imperfect F Type

The three lines come together in one place; and there are numerous fine lines in the palm in this pattern, which is common among women. Such people are usually nervous and frequently shock others with misanthropical or other unusual behavior.

In childhood and youth they are often physically frail and especially afflicted with bronchial and cardiac ailments. But they have good artistic sense and perception and are frequently people of genius. Like the preceding one, the (2) F Type is easily transmitted genetically and has a high likelihood of appearing in twins. People with it tire easily. They fall passionately in love but usually let chances to get married pass them by. In money matters, their fortune is good. They make money easily and tend to be fond of gambling.

(3) Complicated F Type

In this the rarest of the F Types, which occurs in no more than one person in every hundred, all three basic lines overlap; and the entire palm is so crisscrossed with a spider web of lines and creases that the Life, Intellect, and Emotion Lines are indistinguishable. It is found in people with congenital disorders. In childhood, such people are frail and seem to suffer from endocrine illness. They are, however, imaginative and often prove to be geniuses in musical composition or other creative work. They often suffer emotional loss because they are self-giving and self-sacrificing in love. A certain childishness persists in their personalities into adulthood. Women with this type tend to be emotionally disturbed at menstruation time. Newborn infants with this pattern cry at night and do not develop in the normal way.

Classification of Characteristics of Type F

In this pattern, which cuts horizontally across the palm, it is frequent for the Intellect and Emotion Lines to be missing. Type F may therefore be divided into the following three subdivisions (FIG. 40).

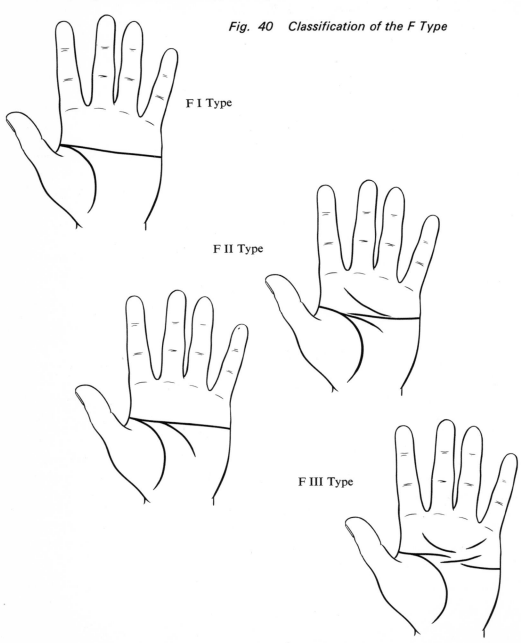

Fig. 40   Classification of the F Type

F I Type

F II Type

F III Type

Type F I
The perfect version in which one simple line cuts straight across the palm and there are few small lines and creases.

Type F II
Either the Intellect or Emotion Line is present with the line cutting straight across the palm. In other words, all three basic lines have come together in one place.

Type F III
Though it cuts straight across, the Emotion Line is irregular because of the presence of many small creases over the entire palm. Furthermore, it is not a single line, but a number of intertwined lines.

Table 7

Emergence Ratios of Type F in Several National and Ethic Groups

	Percentage±m
Swiss	1.2
Dutch	1.5±0.4
Germans	2.8±0.5
Arabs and Berbers	7.9±1.2
Jews	4.6±1.5
Gypsies	14.3±4.7
Eskimos (Greenland)	1.3±1.4
Chinese	13.0±3.4
Pygmies	34.7±2.7

Table 8

General View of Type F (%)

	male	female
primary-school pupils	2.7	2.4
middle-school pupils	3.6	2.3
nursing-school pupils	5.8	4.8
first-year pupils	3.6	2.5
pupils in a Jewish school	4.6	0
breast-feeding infants	3.5	3.0
mentally retarded children	8.6	8.3
epileptics	5.0	5.4
schizophrenics	5.0	5.4
political criminals	5.0	—
other criminals	5.4	—
doctors	2.2	—
lawyers	3.8	—
educators	4.7	3.4

Table 9
Occurrence Frequency of Type F and Modified F Type by Sex
and Body Side (Weininger)

Sex	Number of hands observed		F Type		Modified F Type				III		Total of unusual types	
					IIa		IIb					
	left	right	left	right	left	right	left	right	left	right	left	right
male	115	115	13.9	13.0	—	8.7	7.8	2.6	25.2	20.9	3.5	6.1
female	71	71	14.1	9.9	2.8	4.2	7.0	4.2	21.1	21.1	5.6	5.6
male	33	32	3.0	6.2	3.0	—	—	3.1	21.2	21.9	—	6.2
female	23	23	—	—	4.3	17.4	4.3	4.3	21.7	17.4	4.3	—
male	46	45	2.2	6.7	8.7	11.1	6.5	4.3	17.4	15.6	6.5	6.5
female	30	31	6.7	6.4	13.3	3.2	10.0	—	10.0	16.1	6.7	6.4
male	521	521	3.5	3.3	1.3	1.5	2.1	1.3	19.2	19.0	5.2	4.2
female	557	557	2.0	1.3	0.9	1.3	2.0	2.2	25.7	28.7	2.5	2.0

Genetic Influences

The three basic lines are readily transferable genetically. After having examined the hands of 3,775 infants and of their parents, I have come to the conclusion that the characteristics of the parents' palm patterns are reflected in similar patterns in their children's hands. And Type F, in which a single line crosses the palm horizontally, is the one most susceptible of genetic transmission. Even if only one parent has this so-called *masukake* palm pattern, characterized by two instead of the normal three basic lines, it is highly likely to appear in the children's hands.

Coming to a similar conclusion after examining the hands of 62 families, the German anthropologist H. Schiller said that, when both parents demonstrate it, the *masukake* patterns occurs in the children's hands with more than triple the ordinary rate of probability. When the Life and Intellect Lines of the patterns of both parents overlap at their starting points, it is highly likely that the same characteristic will be manifest in the children's hands too.

In six out of ten cases, when the starting points of these lines are separate in the palms of both parents, they will be separate in the palms of the children. In such instances, children rarely demonstrate either the pattern in which the starting points overlap or the *masukake* pattern.

In 1942, Schiller studied similarity in the palm patterns of twins and learned that in identical twins the similarity was great in 74.4 percent of all cases studies. In fraternal twins, on the other hand the patterns were often different and could be said to resemble each other slightly in only 28.4 percent of the cases studied.

Although as of yet our understanding of the effect of genetic transmission is inadequate, the considerable difference in the occurrence rates of the patterns according to race and region suggests that the influence of heredity is great.

Palm Pattern and Personality

Comparative research between people of the A and D Types, in which the starting points of the Life and Emotion Lines overlap, and those of the B and C Types, in which they do not, reveals that differences in basic palm patterns reflect in clear differences in personality, mental attitude, and physique. Though considerable anthropological study has been made of palm-pattern distribution, at present research on their relation with personality is inadequate. The first to undertake such work, in the 1940's, Charlotte Wolff was active in research on the psychological connections between palm pattern and personality. In her analysis, she found a hint in the system worked out by E. Kretschmer and W. Sheldon, in which personality is correlated to physique types and biological conditions (the science dealing with to this system is referred to as morpho-psychology). From a very early time, the Kretschmer system was generally recognized and used in psychological diagnoses in France and Switzerland. Wolff's simple fleshy hand corresponds to Kretschmer's pyknic type, her motor bony hand to his athletic type, and her long sensitive hand to his leptosomatic type. On the basis of these three basic types, she attempted to discover relations between palmar pattern and personality.

Louis Corman, who is engaged in a most unusual aspect of morpho-psychology, attempts to divine human personality characteristics from facial shape and area. Dividing the face horizontally into three regions, he then investigates developments of the eye, nose, and mouth-and-chin zones. Comparing the areas of the three, he works out a system of two major classifications: the expansive face and the contracted face. From these facial types, he attempts to discover latent personality traits. For instance, people with an expansive face tend to be extroverted and to make their ideas known to others, whereas people with a contracted face easily become introspective.

Work in the field of physiognomy and psychology stimulated research in the psychological implications of the hand. In 1968, in Barcelona, Clement Brun introduced the topic in the First International Conference on the Study of Personality, thus taking the initial forward step in the field since, twenty-four years earlier, Charlotte Wolff had made her research public. To distinguish between this scientific study of the hand and personality from traditional palmistry, he coined the term *chirometrie*.

Palm Pattern and General Personality

AL I Type
When obsessed by something, a person of this nervous, introverted type is unable to turn his attention to anything else. Such people prefer thinking to acting and often demonstrate a mystical spiritual sense. They enjoy traveling and are especially

attracted to mountain and sea scenery. Their perceptions are keen. They are often able to foresee the future. With a giving personality, they do their all for others and tend to be the victims of unrequited love. Not infrequently, the sympathy a man of this type feels for women develops into romantic love. Men of the type tend to be uxorious. Owing to talents in literary expression, they are suited to work in planning and mass communications, though they are slightly negative in relations with other people.

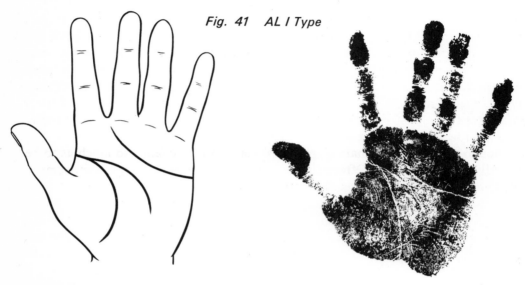

Fig. 41   AL I Type

AL II Type

People with these lovely, slender hands tend to be slim, to have many good ideas, to be skillful at interior decorating and fashion, to have excellent aesthetic sense, and to be generally creative.

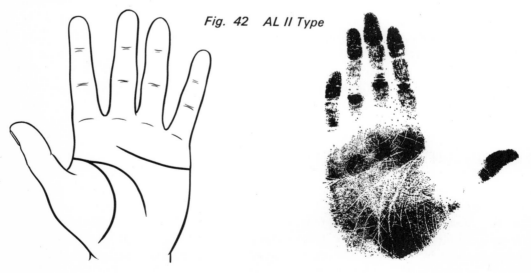

Fig. 42   AL II Type

They have big dreams for the future and have amazing experiences before the age of twenty. They marry either very early or very late. Since they become passionate easily and then cool quickly, for a successful marriage, the partners require some common interest or hobby. These creative people are very talented in such fields as design and television entertainment.

Though they are relatively rare, men with hands of this kind are usually nervous and become enthusiastic about things easily. They are often literarily talented.

AL III Type

People with this kind of hand have high ideals and live under the guidance of their dreams. They are often leaders of such organizations as labor unions. Before the age of thirty, they experience many changes and find it difficult to stay with one job. Women of this type have a hard time finding a marriage partner and remain single until their thirties, at which time they suddenly become popular with men. Frequently such people live for their own great ideals, which may entail such things as social revolution, and devote their energy to service activities.

Though they tend to remain single, once married they change so much as to be virtually different people. Often religious leaders, participants in social movements, or politicians, they are passionate and thorough in all things.

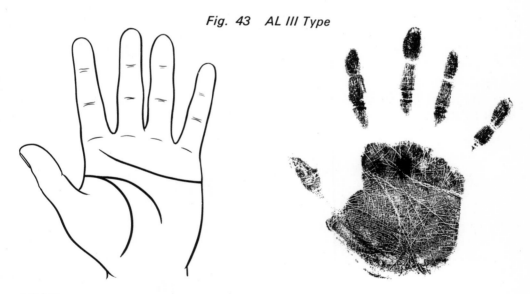

Fig. 43   AL III Type

AO I Type

These people of sound common sense dislike adventure. Though they get along well with others, enjoy helping, and have bright dispositions, they are slightly weak-willed. Prudent and cautious, they tend to live within the bounds of safety. Because, though faithful—often white-collar—workers, they lack leadership and powers of decision and therefore frequently do not make a brilliant place for themselves in the world. Nonetheless, they often succeed as a result of attaining

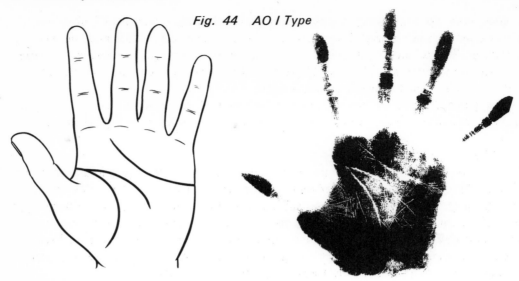

Fig. 44 AO I Type

qualifications in some field of endeavor or of acquiring special talents. An understanding partner or ally can help them expand their abilities.

They find love affairs difficult and, in Japan at any rate, prefer arranged marriages. They are home-bodies and doting parents. They are safer avoiding change and working steadily at their own pace since they run into danger if they attempt to rush things. Lacking courage, on the job and at home, they put safety first. Such people are outstanding at clerical work or accounting.

AO II Type

Men with this type of hand are prone to violent emotional ups and downs and often undergo drastic personality changes in the teens and twenties. They become

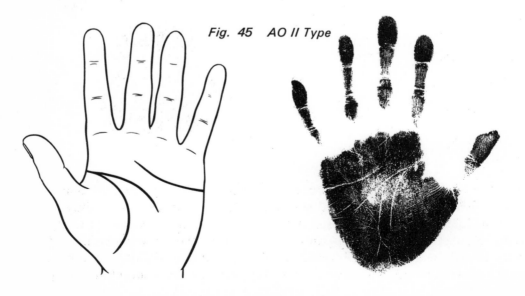

Fig. 45 AO II Type

angry easily. One of their greatest difficulties is a tendency to partiality in personal relations.

Though they are often beautiful with especially lovely eyes, women of this type tend to be hysterical. Because of their charm they are always made much of by others. Their preferences in men are violent. Since they tend to give completely, they not infrequently sacrifice themselves for worthless men. They have a chance for a great love affair before they are twenty-five.

These people tend to undergo considerable emotional fluctuations at about the month of their birthday. Women of this kind are more than usually disturbed at menstruation time. Continuing in the same work for more than three years bores them since they constantly seek new stimulation. Because of their strong originality and creativity, they are suited to design or other artistic work.

AO III Type

These people are strong-willed and tenacious. While seemingly calm and cool, they are capable of bold deeds and great courage. They display their best side in organizations because of their talents in politics and leadership. Often they succeed no matter what kind of work they undertake and frequently become bosses. Slightly selfish in love and marriage, they are often misunderstood and counted cold because they are slow to show their feelings. Women of this kind seem especially chilly and appear stronger than men. Even when they fall in love with someone, they maintain calm.

Their considerable talents mature late. Though perhaps not especially brilliant, they can succeed in a course of action demanding brilliance. Many of them are big-businessmen or politicians or engage in other fields where they can manifest their powers. Given an opportunity, they throw themselves completely into the

Fig. 46   AO III Type

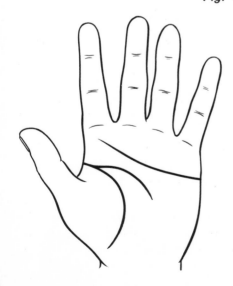

task at hand. They are well suited to business because of their powers of leadership and judgment and because of their ability to make an impression.

AH I Type

Reticent and active, with interest and ability in sports, such people faithfully carry out all work given them; but, because they pay little or no attention to small matters, they make frequent errors. They have many friends on the job and like and are able to drink. Home is the center of their lives. They prefer safety and judge things optimistically. As has been said, they pay little attention to minor matters and are refreshing and candid in personality.

Women of this type are strong-willed and can do any kind of work with better than normal success. Their personalities stabilize in the thirties and forties. Ideally they should do sports- or computer-related work.

Fig. 47   AH I Type

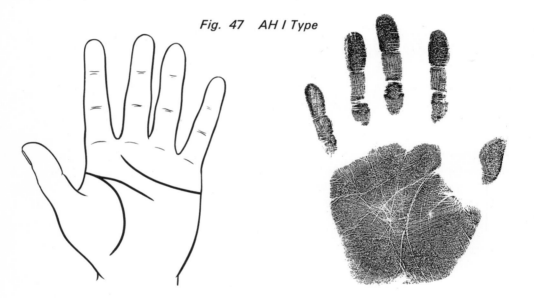

AH II Type

Self-centered and unwilling to lose, these strong people have great powers of action and decisiveness. This type is frequent in women, especially women who are conspicuous in business or other organizations. They can easily be uncooperative and tend to be preferential in their friendships. In work and love, they are unsatisfied by the ordinary and are always on the move in search of new things. Their marriages frequently fail because they require far more than is reasonable from their spouses. Women of this type are not ideally suited to the role of wife for an ordinary white-collar worker, though they are exactly right as the wife of a leader in big business or of an entertainer. Men of this type make excellent motion-picture directors or television producers and work successfully in television commercials.

Fig. 48   AH II Type

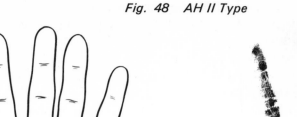

AH III Type
Bold and audacious, these people do not care that they are disliked for being overpowering and for acting without taking the opinions and needs of others into consideration. They are the kinds of men who are presidents of medium and small businesses and who establish a family fortune in one generation. Though women find them very dependable, philandering is one of their major faults and a frequent source of trouble.

Fig. 49   AH III Type

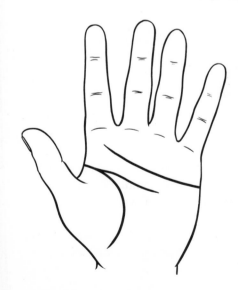

Women of this type tend to be cold and at first uninterested in sex. They often run away from their husbands on the wedding night. Once interested in it, however, they become more than ordinarily captivated by sex. They have very clear preferences in men and will under no circumstances show favor to someone who is not their type. They are strongly interested in money, which, for some of them, is the sole criterion of value.

BL I Type

This is the fanciful, dreamy type that is very little interested in reality but, fond of literature, poetry, and music, can become infatuated with the heros and heroines of novels and motions pictures. Always frustrated, these people are constantly seeking thrills. Men of this kind are attracted to older women, and women of the type are drawn to younger men. More interested in their work than in marital life, they generally marry late and usually show ability in artistic endeavors like television entertaining, modeling, or writing novels.

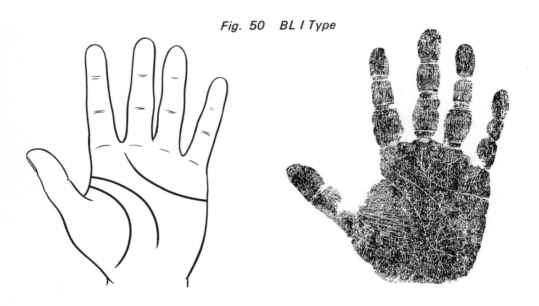

Fig. 50   BL I Type

BL II Type

Emotional and determined to win, both men and women of this type show pleasure and displeasure at once in their facial expressions. They have distinctively shaped mouths. Women are unforgettable because of their individual charm. Confident of face and figure, they are frequently active as fashion models or television entertainers. Quickly aroused, they are often loved by men considerably older than they. This is the type that produces great actresses and motion-picture stars.

Fig. 51   BL II Type

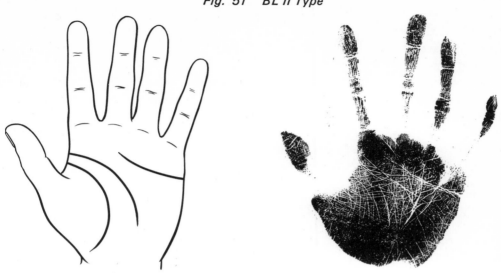

BL III Type

These people tend to be sad and emotionally uneven and to seek adventure and thrills. Interested in many things, they quickly become enthusiastic and equally as quickly cool off. Women of this type require the devotion of men and are very possessive. In sex, they are passionate and learn to savor sexual pleasure at an early age.

Men of this type are outstandingly talented—even geniuses—in art and often tend to lose themselves in fantasy.

Fig. 52   BL III Type

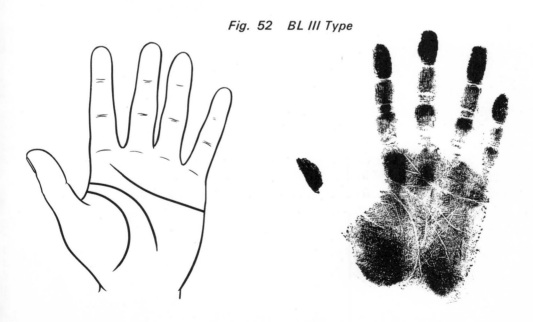

BO I Type

Both men and women of this type are active and determined to win. Though they dislike defeat, they have the bigness to take the opinions of others into consideration before acting. This pattern occurs frequently in women who are of the first-daughter type.

They generally do better in active work—like sales—than in more modest undertakings—like office work. Their marriages are usually romantic and not arranged, their proposals are persistent: they will not give in until the partner agrees to the marriage. That is why they sometimes marry extraordinarily beautiful women. Often their courtships are brief and dramatic; they brook no objections. Stubbornness is the salient characteristic of their personalities.

Fig. 53   BO I Type

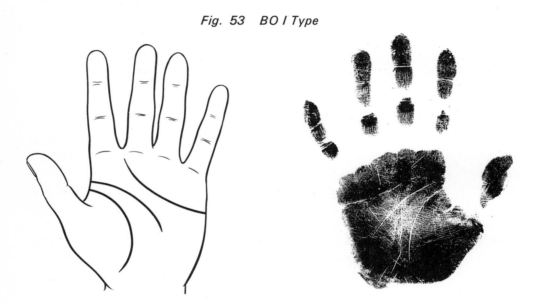

BO II Type

Passion governs each day of people belonging in this type. They live and die for love. Unable to tolerate halfway measures in work or romance, when they fall in love, they are capable of giving up everything for it. The majority of women of this type run the danger of losing their virginity before they are twenty. They are the kind who always act before they think. They stand out and are discontent with the ordinary. Many women of the type continue working after marriage. Men tend to be successful in politics and business, though they have many rivals.

Fig. 54 BO II Type

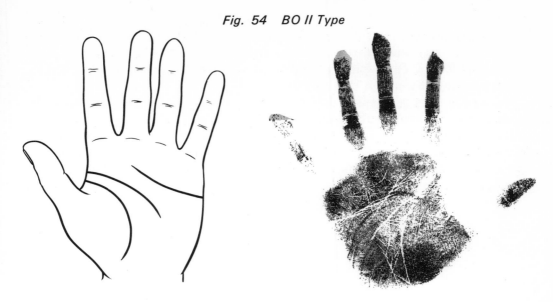

BO III Type

People of this type are adventurous and deliberately seek novelty. They think more of the future than of the past and sometimes shock people with their bold actions.

Highly active and slightly stubborn, they often succeed as politicians and businessmen. Their life-styles vary frequently in their twenties. In their forties, however, they become good at amassing money. They plan and calculate closely and tend to work on their own. When they fail, it is on a big scale. But the same can be said of their successes. Since they have great talent in politics, they are frequently leaders in military or political affairs or in such organizations as labor unions.

Fig. 55 BO III Type

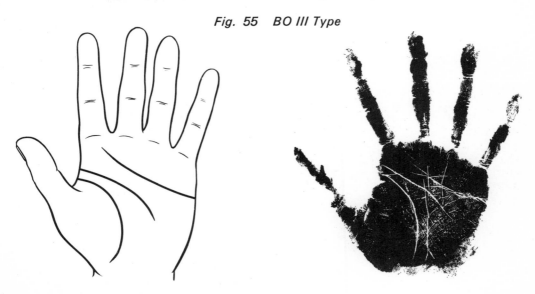

BH I Type

These people are understanding and quickly put their decisions into practice. Sociable and lively, they have the makings of unfailing popularity. But, since their likes and dislikes in companions are pronounced, they change completely when in the company of someone they find distasteful.

Men and women of this type tend to prefer romantic to arranged marriages and succeed in sales or commercial work.

They have a sense of responsibility and enthusiastically give their all for a person they like. Because they are good at making money they can succeed in business and are well suited to the management of bars, restaurants, or similar service-oriented endeavors.

Fig. 56   BH I Type

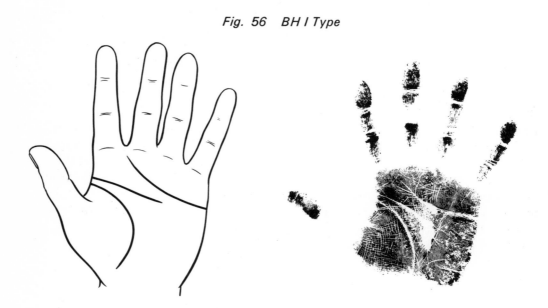

BH II Type

Fond of change, these people have high ideals and like to win. Their quick temper is a failing. Though members of the same sex tend to dislike them, they are very popular with members of the opposite sex. Since they are hard workers, they frequently succeed. Men of this type display great ability in accounting and law; women, in secretarial and consultant work. In romance, failure to understand the partner's personality can lead to trouble.

Fig. 57   BH II Type

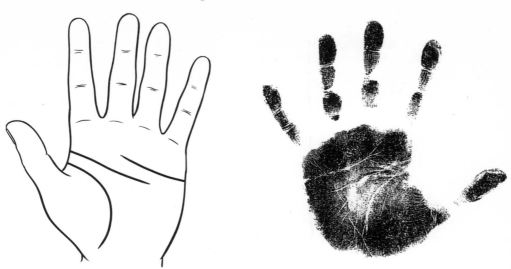

BH III Type

This, the most masculine and virile of the hand patterns, is found in men with sturdy, strong bodies. Women find them attractive, but they show little interest. They succeed in such masculine roles as pilots and sportsmen. These reliable people cause no money trouble; but, because their subordinates and juniors rely on them, their many visitors can be a problem for the housewife.

Women with this hand are stronger than many men and succeed in business or politics, in which they are often elected to public office.

Fig. 58   BH III Type

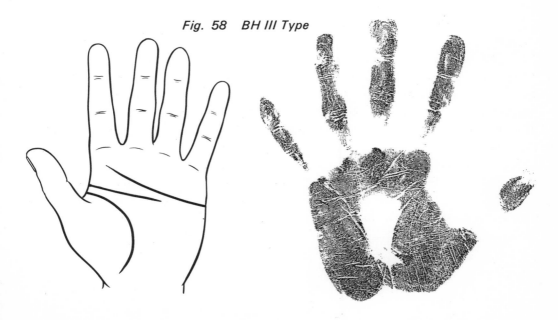

CL I Type

This rare pattern is found in people who are dreamy, fantasizers discontent with actuality and often irritable. Traveling or a change of scene should give them more courage, which they require. In work too, they must avoid monotony and seek change and variety. They prefer arranged to romantic marriages and usually find a good partner relatively early. They should select spouses whose personalities are the opposite of their own.

Fig. 59   CL I Type

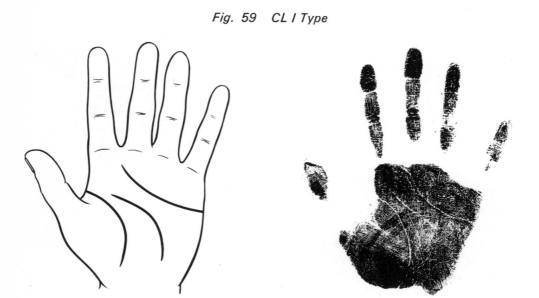

CL II Type

Men and women of this type are good with their hands, have many excellent ideas, persevere, and tend to become wrapped up in the things that interest them. They are suited to the medical and pharmacological professions. Very romantic, they exert their fullest efforts for the sake of members of the opposite sex; and their attentions frequently develop into marriage. They are attracted to people who are their physical opposites.

Married women of this kind are never content to be idle and frequently have their own work, which varies and stimulates both partners' life-style.

Fig. 60   CL II Type

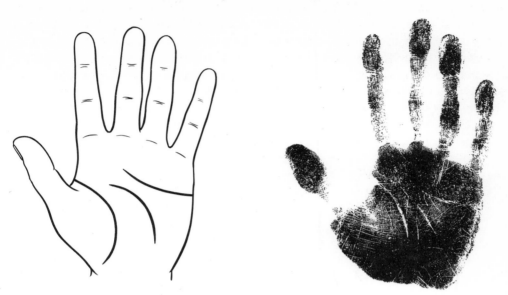

CL III Type

Found once in ten thousand people, this unusual pattern occurs in extreme types —fool or genius—especially in mathematical theory. Albert Einstein's hand was of this pattern. Such people are relatively unaware of women and are uninterested in anything but lofty love affairs. They tend to prefer arranged marriages. For them, married life centers on work and bears fruit in late years.

Fig. 61   CL III Type

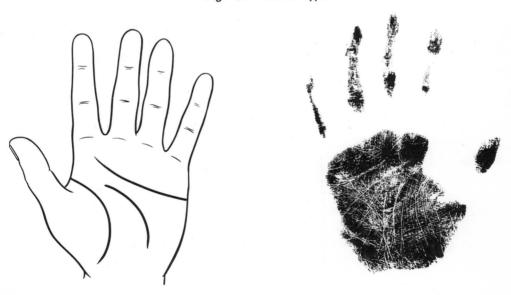

CO I Type

People of this type frequently have good ideas and startle others with their unusual behavior. But they have the failing of tending to act without taking results into consideration. They are certain to succeed if they are headed in the right direction but must be extremely cautious to avoid wrong directions, to which they are prone.

This pattern is especially frequent in inventors, research workers, and other roles in which making the best of special ideas is important.

In love, they give themselves entirely without looking ahead. Separating people into the kinds they like and the kinds they do not, they never associate with others on the basis of premeditated calculation and therefore frequently fall blindly in love.

They tend to marry easily without paying much attention to physical appearance and lead calm lives, devoted to spouse and children.

Fig. 62   CO I Type

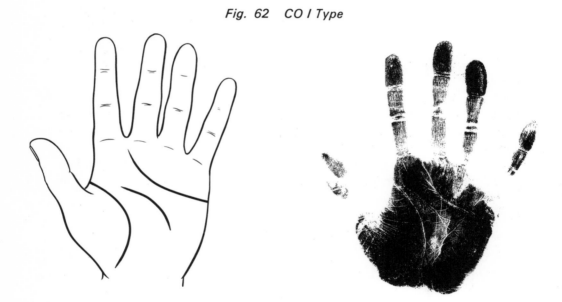

CO II Type

This hand pattern is so rare that it occurs in less than one in ten thousand. Such people tend to give up easily, to be irritable, and to fret. They can develop their individuality and make a way for themselves through educating their abilities. Since physical weakness aggravates their situation, it is important that they strengthen themselves as much as possible. Further they must attempt to develop the courage to overcome difficulties. Some people of this type have succeeded in music by correctly cultivating their inner beings.

Romance is difficult for them. They tend to rely on and idolize others. Arranged marriage is suitable, and they should choose a partner of a type opposite to their own: AH III, BO III, or BH III.

Fig. 63   CO II Type

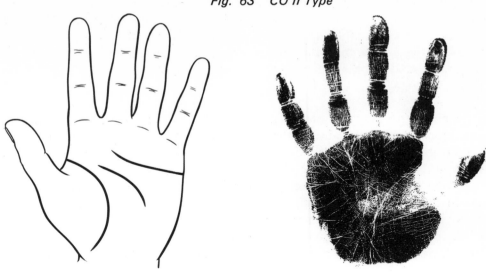

CO III Type

This pattern occurs in people who have the perseverance to continue studying and working on a problem till they have elucidated something previously unknown. Scholars, doctors, and university professors manifest it often. A failing of these people is a tendency to explode emotionally when dissatisfied.

In romance, they are irresolute and do not make their intentions clearly known. Often they marry after a long courtship, though these affairs frequently drag on too long and end in tears.

Fig. 64   CO III Type

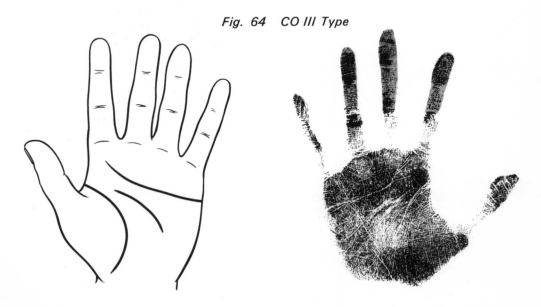

Men of this type prefer women much younger than themselves, and women tend to marry men greatly their seniors. Domestic life is placid, though men of this type tend to philander, especially with women of a type different from that of their wives. The forties are the most dangerous time for extramarital affairs. Women of this type are said to be self-giving, good wives and mothers.

CH I Type

Many people of this kind are interested in many things and cannot be satisfied with one alone. Perhaps because of their deliberateness and multitude of interests, they tend to be unfaithful. They often attempt two jobs at once or change occupations easily.

In love they prefer number. From a large group of people of the opposite sex, they gradually select one with whom to fall passionately in love and then marry, practically before they know it themselves. In their thirties, however, their attitude toward the opposite sex alters suddenly. Married life too usually becomes happier after they have entered their thirties. Thereafter, their expectations are good.

Fig. 65   CH I Type

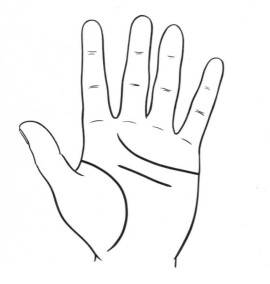 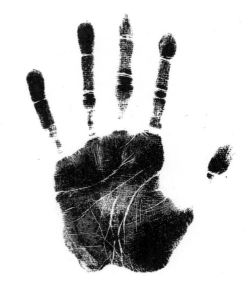

CH II Type

Though rare, this pattern, which occurs with some frequency in artists, is found in high-strung, gloomy people who think too deeply about things. It is imperative for them to overcome themselves and to find good conversational companions and friends with sunny dispositions.

Their love is frequently unrequited and secret. They prefer arranged marriages. Married life for them is more stable and happier if they have children early.

Fig. 66   CH II Type

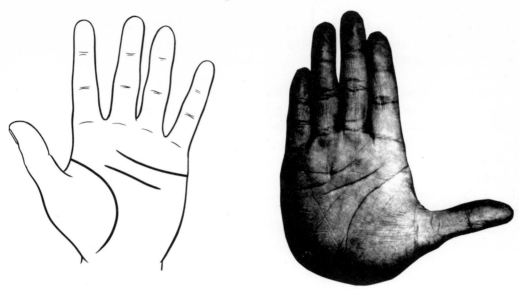

CH III Type

This pattern is rare in women and belongs to active, forceful men who are leaders in any age and who become highly independent as a result of hardships in youth. In love, they are extremely persistent. Women in whom the pattern does occurs should be on their guard since their strong personalities can make other people shun them. In married life, men of this type are completely reliable and approach the ideal masculine image.

Fig. 67   CH III Type

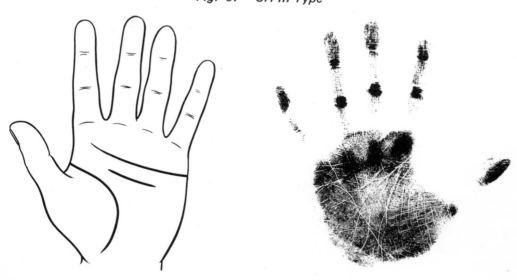

DL I Type

These people are extremely introverted, lack decisiveness, and sooner or later suffer mentally. But, very romantic, they have great powers of imagination, often come up with ideas unthinkable to ordinary people, and have wonderful spiritual gifts. Poetically and literarily talented, they are ideally suited to religious work or counselling.

In romance, their affections are often unrequited. In general, they prefer Platonic relations. Lacking in sexual energy, they are good technically.

Men and women of this kind often fail in love because they express their affections too soon. Married life is better if the spouses are close to each other in age and stabilizes in middle age. Women of this kind are completely faithful to their husbands.

Fig. 68   DL I Type

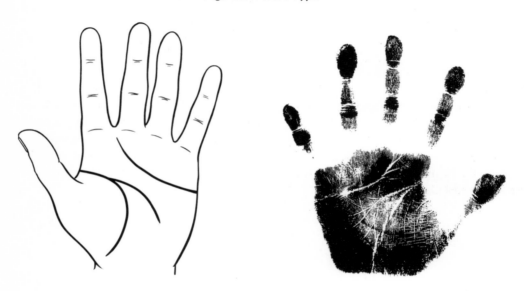

DL II Type

Women of this type are very beautiful, with especially lovely profiles and eyes, and enjoy great popularity with men. But they often miss important chances by being obsessed with certain ideas or by fretting. They are artistically very sensitive and pay close attention to their clothes and cosmetics. They devote much thought to the decoration of their rooms. Weakness for men, especially handsome men, is one of their great faults; and they have such great feminine devotion that they are willing to sacrifice their lives for the men they love. In matters related to love and marriage, they should heed the advice of others instead of acting on their own. Sometimes they have unhappy love affairs before the age of twenty-five.

Fig. 69   DL II Type

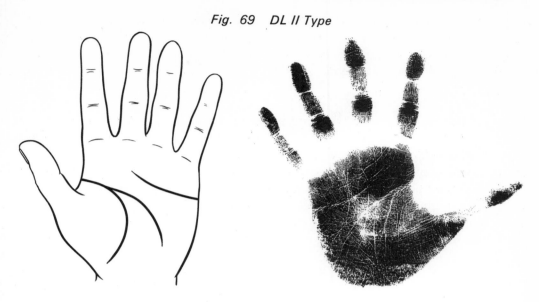

DL III Type

People of this nervous, introverted type are often misunderstood because it is diffi-cult to know what is on their minds. They are, however, intelligent and talented. Because they are reliable and active, they do well as workers in banks or securities firms and are very successful if they have good superiors. They display better-than-average powers in whatever work they undertake and are trusted by people in positions of authority. Once they are disliked, however, it is difficult for them to eliminate the misunderstanding behind their lack of popularity. They tend to have difficulty with human relations. They have many interests and are strongly drawn

Fig. 70   DL III Type

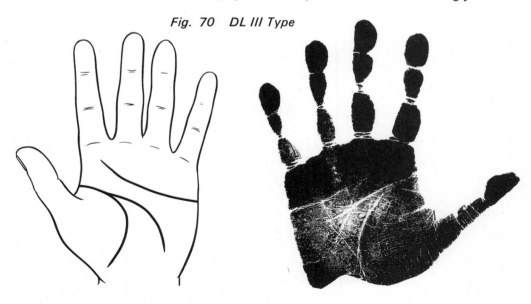

to literature, music, painting, and other fields of artistic endeavor. In love, they can be misunderstood since they are cool and reluctant to show their feelings. It is to the advantage of men of this type to marry in their twenties. Women too enjoy a stable life if they marry early.

DO I Type
People in this most standard type tend to be slightly nervous and introverted. They do nothing excessively dramatic, are quiet and diligent, and dislike adventure. Maturing late, though they may have made only moderate grades in school, they frequently demonstrate brilliance when they turn what had been a hobby or a part-time job into a full-time occupation. They are ordinary in love but give their partners faithfulness and reliability. Owing to a lack of perseverance, they can suffer unhappiness in love affairs. People of this type are accommodating and work well in public offices, banks, or commercial enterprises.

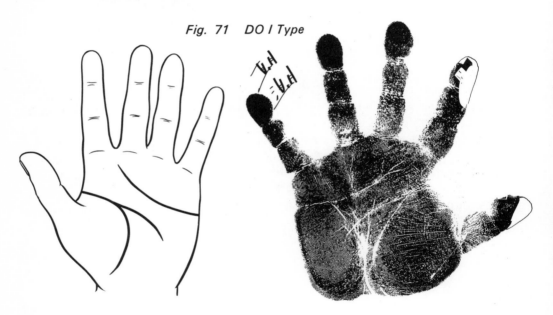

Fig. 71   DO I Type

DO II Type
Women of this irritable and fretting type tend to be slightly hysterical. They quickly become enthusiastic over beautiful and new things but equally as quickly cool off. Love affairs go well for the first six months, after which trouble sets in. Then the partner's feelings change, or the DO II person becomes interested in some other member of the opposite sex. Romantic marriages have a high success rate, but in arranged marriages such people have a hard time finding the right partner.

Men of this type are suited to work in advertising, publishing, and photography; women, to work in handicrafts, music, or such fields as flower arrangement in which they can put their artistic sensibilities to good use.

Fig. 72   DO II Type

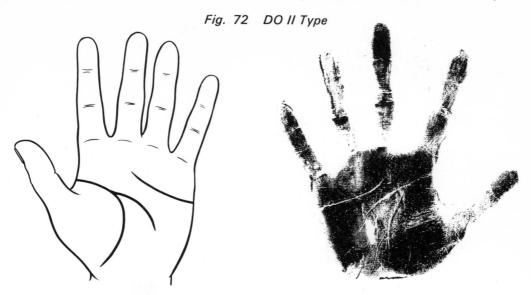

DO III Type

People with this palm pattern have the highest success rates of all and tend to be executives in any company, where they are trusted by seniors and juniors alike. They plan for the future and are highly intelligent. Acquiring special qualifications, gives them a chance to demonstrate still more power.

In spite of their reliability and determination to win, women of this type tend to be shunned by men and frequently have the fault of never making an effort to smile. Because of their positive personalities, many of them succeed with arranged marriages. Although their married life is stable, both sexes tend to give precedence to work. With a talent for savings, investments, and planning, they know how to make money.

Fig. 73   DO III Type

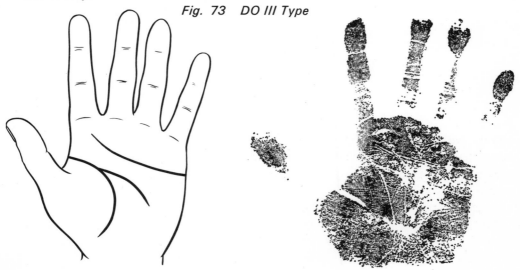

DH I Type

Often people of this type have frank, bright personalities, are mentally acute, and make rational judgments. Men of this type succeed in law and medicine or are often inventors and discoverers. Women are often teachers or doctors.

Uncomplicated in love, they do not fret and rarely become passionate. Because of their devotion to research and work, they often marry late and then usually, where such is the custom, by arrangement. They are happiest when their spouses are employed in the same kind of work and are on the same level of intelligence as they.

Fig. 74   DH I Type

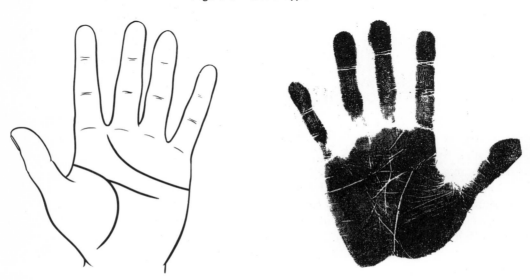

DH II Type

This type occurs often in men. Such people are talented and intelligent and have both many good ideas and the initiative to put them into practice. For this reason, they follow an elite course of advancement in the business world.

Such people became famous in society as well as on the job and tend to have an innovating influence on both spheres. Their occupation frequently changes drastically in their thirties.

In love, they are passionate and give their all to the person they select. Men of this type are frequently attracted by older women. After marriage, philandering is often a danger.

Women in this type tend to succeed as bar hostesses or in the service sector of society.

Fig. 75   DH II Type

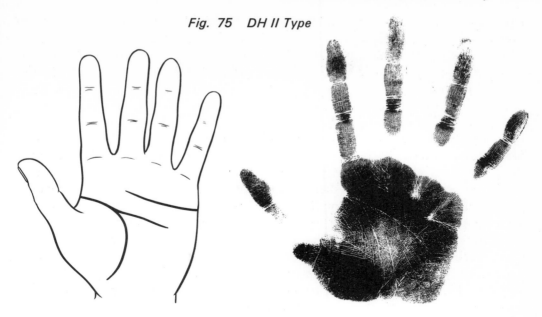

DH III Type

Though apparently mild-mannered, these people can be very bold. They tend to have the fight to see work through without being discouraged by one or two failures. Among people of this type are many who, in spite of lack of good fortune in youth, seize their chance for success in business, technical fields, or art and entertainment when they are nearly thirty. Shy and hesitant to express their feel-

Fig. 76   DH III Type

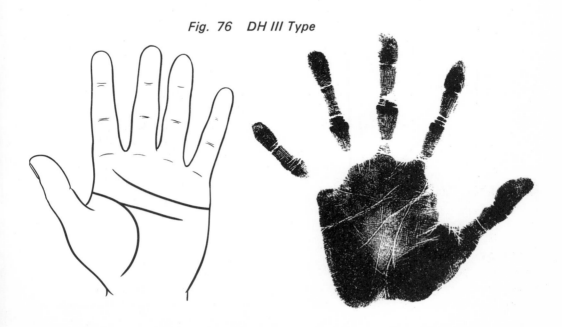

ings, they often have unsuccessful love affairs. Husbands of this type are sometimes slightly selfish and domineering. Women of this type too tend to be very strong-willed. They display their powers from their twenties to their forties. And, because they are more talented than their husbands, such women often become the centers of their families.

EL I Type

Intelligent but extremely introverted, people of this type are romanticists who prefer being wrapped in their own thoughts, listening to music or reading, to anything else. They like a quiet environment and hate loud talking, shouting, or other coarse behavior, which causes them a degree of distress unimaginable to ordinary people. They remember anything that gets on their nerves for a very long time. They are popular with everyone because of their faithfulness and the way they get along well with and take an interest in the welfare of others. Old people tend to make much over them.

Artistically talented and with abundant powers of intuition and imagination, they do well in such fields as illustration and animation or the design of floral creations, jewelry, or clothing. In addition, they can put their romantic tendencies to good use in the writing of children's stories. Good voices stand them in good stead in singing or in announcing. In addition, they can put their literary abilities to good use in the publishing field.

Fig. 77 EL I Type

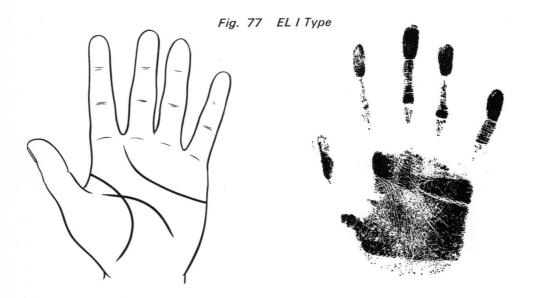

EL II Type

Gentle and considerate, these people have rich imaginations and artistic talents and are extremely sensitive to beautiful things. They are sometimes delicate dreamers, preferring the world of fantasy to reality. But, owing to their extremely refined nerves, they are upset by and suffer because of very insignificant matters. Similarly they are easily irritated and excited. Their great caution sometimes robs them of decisiveness. Artistic talent and powers of expression suit them well to all expressive fields, including *ikebana*, the tea ceremony, and the profession of the beautician. Characterized by linguistic abilities, they are suited to jobs as translators, interpreter-guides, and airline hostesses.

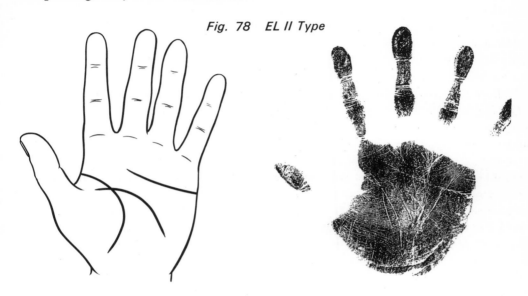

Fig. 78 EL II Type

EL III Type

These people tend to experience violent manic-depressive emotional differences at home and on the job and should therefore always strive to maintain a cool, stable condition. In love too, their emotions come to the forefront, making them

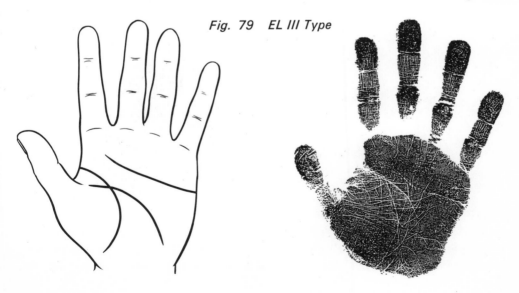

Fig. 79 EL III Type

quick to become blindly passionate and then quick to cool off. After marriage, however, they settle down as harmonious, reliable people if they find the right kind of partner. Since they are easily influenced, if they marry a worthless person, the marriage is likely to fail. In other words, the right spouse is extremely important for people of this type.

Their abundant talents, overflowing creativity, and great originality suit them to work requiring good ideas, to free-lance work, and to creative and artistic work. Furthermore, they are gifted with the ability to put their ideas to use in financial matters.

EO I Type

These people are introverted, are slightly nervous, and prefer speculative thought to action. They are sensitive enough to perceive acutely the thoughts of others. Very considerate of members of the opposite sex, they tend to devote themselves entirely to their sweethearts. In Japan, where the practice is fairly common, young men of this type are frequently asked to marry into families by adoption. Because of their considerate nature, such people often allow sympathy to develop into love, marry people of entirely different backgrounds, and continue kind and considerate after marriage. They succeed in work that puts to good use their strong powers of imagination and keen intuition. Many of them are literarily talented and are perfectly suited to work connected with the mass-communications media. Since they have tastes in harmony with modern times, their futures are bright.

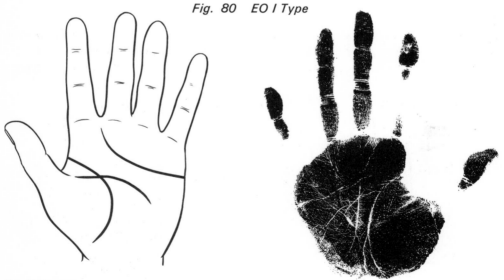

Fig. 80 EO I Type

EO II Type

Though emotionally unstable, such people, who are slightly nervous, can become extremely enthusiastic about things to which they turn their attention. They can, however, become so wrapped up in something that they fret and let good chances pass them by. With a little more positive initiative, they can develop into excellent people. In love too, they worry and are delighted or grieved by the least change in their partner's behavior. With classic appeal, they can be extremely popular, though they tend to lack fight. With the stability of married life, they settle down completely. Making full use of their great creativity and abundant ideas enables them to grow. They should select occupations that emerge from hobbies or that demand specialist knowledge. Men of this type have a high rate of success in work oriented toward women.

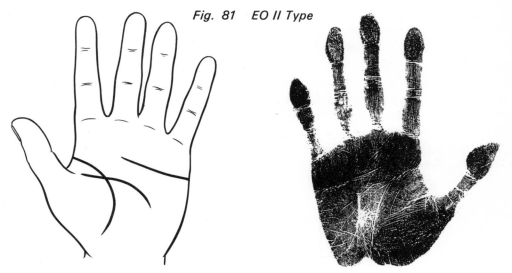

Fig. 81   EO II Type

EO III Type

Unsatisfied with the commonplace, these people have a powerful desire to be seen and are interested in many things, including music, literature, and painting. They are very intelligent and highly understanding and demonstrate distinctive powers

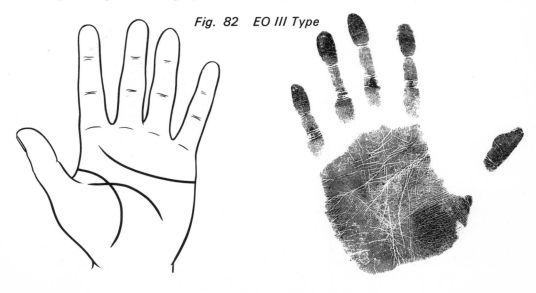

Fig. 82   EO III Type

in anything they undertake. But they are chilly in personal relations and tend to give an unsociable impression. Men of this type generally marry late but make considerate, reliable husbands.

These people are so talented in so many things that it is difficult to tell what their main occupation is. After changing from one field to another, they tend to manifest even greater powers than before and are best suited to occupations demanding great ability.

EH I Type

Everyone likes people of this type, who have bright, serious dispositions and can get along with practically anyone. Blessed with sound common sense, they tend to be somewhat conservative, never take risks, and have no great fondness for adventure. But their strong sense of responsibility makes it impossible for them to treat lightly anything they have undertaken. People rely on them because they always fulfill whatever tasks they are given. Some of the occupations in which they may succeed include educational counsellor, operator, typist, guide, and stenographer. They are certain to do more than average work in literary or scientific fields if they have an interest in them. Others of their characteristics are good motor nerves and extreme bodily and digital agility.

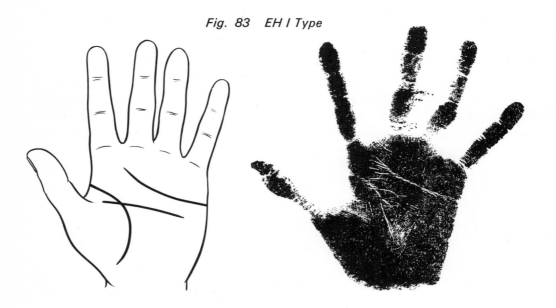

Fig. 83   EH I Type

EH II Type

These people are very sensitive and strongly attracted to beauty. Passionately fond of the lovely and the novel, they rush to be the first to wear the latest fashions but assimilate them so well that they never look odd or strange in them. Their interest in decorating inspires them to create distinctive, original interiors. The aesthetic sense they possess keeps these charming people constantly in the center of attention.

But they tend to be fickle and to allow their present passions to cool quickly. Their artistic sense suits them perfectly to the work of illustrators, painters, animators, and beauticians. They are suited to book design and interior design as well.

Fig. 84   EH II Type

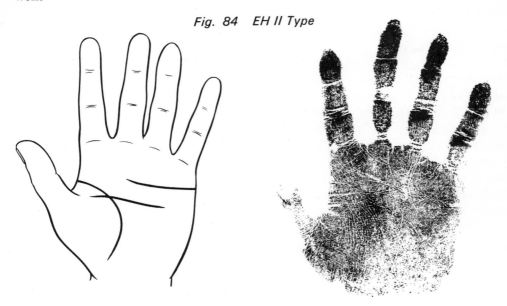

EH III Type
These people are always working for the realization of their big dreams. Though apparently calm and reserved, they have great courage and the initiative to enable them to manifest astounding practical power when the need arises. But they can

Fig. 85   EH III Type

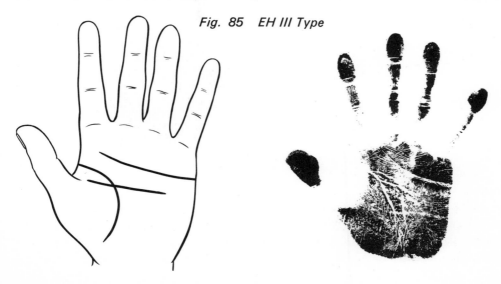

live in harmony with anyone because, under ordinary circumstances, they are gentle, thoughtful, kind, and devoid of irritating characteristics. In any kind of work, they perform accurately and with above-average powers. They are trusted by their associates, owing to their leadership powers and decisiveness and a strong will that enables them to see all tasks through to completion. They work vigorously and with talent and can manifest their powers if they acquire specialist techniques. Suitable occupations include stenographer, magazine journalist, case worker, educational counsellor, administrative dietician, diet and hygiene supervisor, public prosecutor, and so on.

F I Type

Easily transferred hereditarily and frequent in families of genius, this hand pattern often occurs in technicians, doctors, engineers, and scholars. On the surface ordinary, such people are usually courageous, popular, and beloved. Generally they have the genius to be first in their class from the time of primary school. They do well in any work they undertake. The hand of Tokugawa Ieyasu (1542–1616), one of the greatest political figures in Japanese history, was of this pattern.

But such people often suffer because it is difficult for them to find marriage partners. They usually marry late: in the thirties for men and the late twenties for women. They make excellent drivers and are well suited to mechanical work or tasks requiring manual techniques.

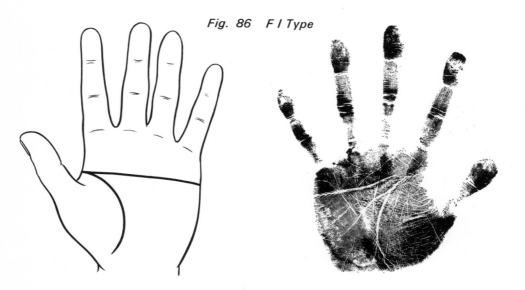

Fig. 86   F I Type

F II Type

This pattern is rare even among the F Types. People with it are often frail from childhood and have weak constitutions. But they have many excellent ideas, put their extraordinary taste to good use, and are often geniuses in musical composition and other creative work.

Devoted in love, they sacrifice themselves for members of the opposite sex and sometimes suffer loss as an outcome. Always preserving a certain childishness, women of this type are violently emotionally upset at about the time of menstruation. Newborn babies with this pattern cry at night and do not develop as well as they should.

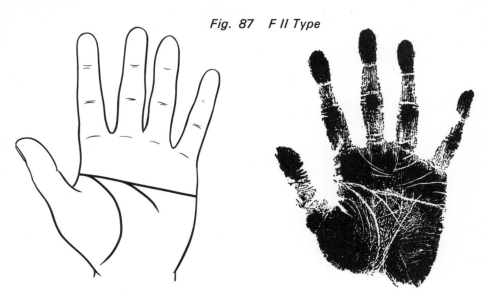

Fig. 87   F II Type

F III Type

This pattern is seen often in women. But both men and women with it are nervous, have violent likes and dislikes in human relations, sometimes suffer from insomnia, and are emotionally inconsistent. They have an artistic flair and are sensitive to

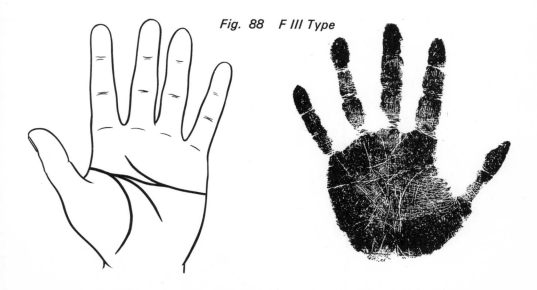

Fig. 88   F III Type

beauty. They are good at singing and other kinds of entertainment and often become famous in such fields.

Like the FI Type readily transmitted hereditarily, this pattern appears with a high rate of frequency in twins. Tiring easily, people with it often suffer from weak respiratory systems.

Passionate in love, they hesitate to marry and often miss good opportunities for this reason. They are strong in money matters, skillful at making profits, and often gambling geniuses.

3. Practical Palm Reading

Viewed in a cursory manner, the four hand patterns in FIG. 89 seem to resemble each other; but a closer examination shows differences. In (A) and (B) creases are few and tend to be long, deep, and clear. The palm is virtually free of the kinds of fine lines seen in (C) and (D). (A) and (B) are male and (C) and (D) female hands. Women's palms generally reveal more fine lines, whereas men's have few creases, which are simple and linear. In (A) and (B), the thumbs are thick and strong and the Mounts of the Moon at their bases are well developed. A still closer look shows that the patterns of lines in the skin of the palms—a pattern similar in nature to fingerprints—are different in all four.

Fig. 89   Hand forms and fingerprints of the index fingers of four people

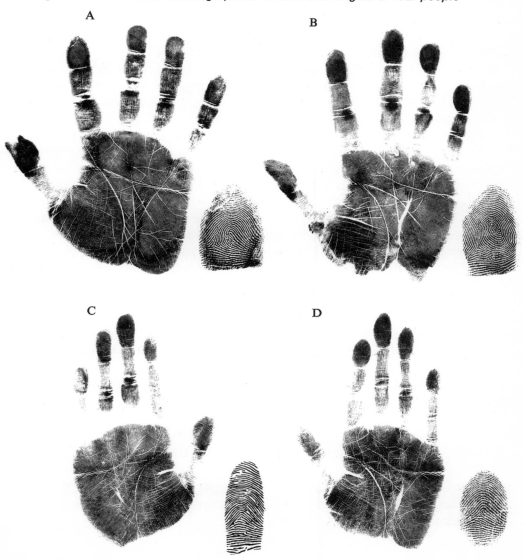

In (A) and (B)—the male—palms, the creases are widely and clearly spaced. When prints are taken of a palm like these, the white and black areas are distinct. In female hands, the spacing among creases is narrow; and, in prints, the white and black areas are interwoven. This is another indication of the clear sex-related differences in hand forms and creases.

But there are still further differences among the patterns of these four hands. The fingerprint of the index finger of (A) has wavelike curves called loops. That of the index finger of (B) demonstrates what are called whorls. And that of (C), while similar to the one in (A), demonstrates what are called arches. The print of the index finger in (D) resembles that in (A) except that the lines flow in a different direction: the heads of the loops are oriented toward the little finger; whereas in (A) they are oriented toward the thumb. As is true in practically everything, a close examination makes possible interesting discoveries in things we see everyday without paying attention to them. Still more interesting things will emerge from a look at the lengths of the fingers and the shapes of the palms.

Whereas in some people the index and ring fingers are practically the same length, in others the index finger is considerably longer. In some people the little finger will fall below, in others will extend above, and in still others will terminate precisely at a line drawn horizontal at the first phalanx of the ring finger.

As to the shape of the palm, in solid-looking (A) it is practically square and is well fleshed. Though the hand is that of a man, in (B), the palm is rectangular and slender. In female (C), the palm is long and slender; and the hypothenar is thin and better shaped than in (D). In (D), a roundish, small hand, the palm is almost square.

These individual differences in palm shape can be connected with differences in physique and facial shape. (A) is the rugged sportsman type with a squarish face and developed chin. (B) is thin with an egg-shaped head and a slender chin. (C) is a tall willowy woman with a well-balanced, slender face. (D) is a small woman with a round face. In general, the shape of the palm, when inverted, is close in configuration to that of the face.

Investigation of the three basic lines—Life, Intellect, and Emotion—of their palm patterns clarifies more differences among these four people. Examining hand patterns is easier if the person performing it knows the various pattern types.

Personality Judged on the Basis of Finger Length

Thumb (Intellect, Will, and Initiative) and Index Finger

Hold the thumb and index finger together, straight. Imagine a line (a) dividing the first phalange of the index finger in half and determine where the tip of your thumb falls in relation to it (FIG. 90).

Fig. 90   Comparison of the lengths of the thumb and index finger

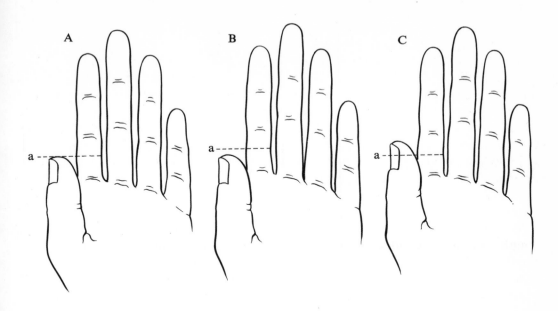

(A)   Terminates exactly at (a)
This is the most ordinary length. People with it understand their position in the world, exert themselves to a suitable degree, are frequently positive and active, and judge things coolly and accurately.

(B)   Terminates below (a)
People with this kind of short thumb are often gentle or weak and hesitate to exert themselves. They lack sticking power and change their minds often. The short thumb is frequent in people who judge matters largely on the basis of intuition.

(C)   Terminates above (a)
People of this type are strong-willed and have great self-respect. They are capable of tremendous fighting power and have a strong desire to command others. Naturally, they dislike taking orders.

Index Finger (Self-respect, Desire for Glory, and Selfishness) and Ring Finger (Artistic and Aesthetic Sensitivity)

Judging the length of the index finger is done in relation to the ring finger (FIG. 91). With all the fingers stretched out straight, compare the lengths of the ring and index fingers.

Fig. 91   Comparison of the lengths of the index and ring fingers

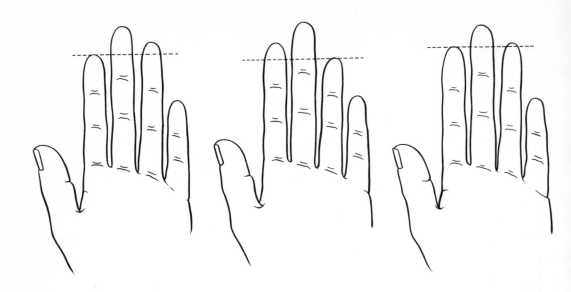

(D)   Index finger slightly shorter than ring finger
This is the most commonly encountered type. Since they take others into consideration as they act in their own interests, people with it rarely encounter friction. They do not take risks and in general lead well-ordered lives.

(E)   Index finger longer than ring finger
People of this type detest losing. They are active and have considerable political ability. They are independent and enjoy assuming positions of leadership.

(F)   Index finger roughly the same length as ring finger
These people dislike anything that is ordinary. Their likes and dislikes in acquaintances are clear. They are possessive and jealous. Since they are very hesitant to expose their true feelings, other people frequently claim to find them inscrutable.

(G)   Ring finger considerably longer
Such people have excellent artistic taste and are imaginative. Weak-willed, they frequently do what others tell them to do. They have individual ideas, are keenly perceptive, and tend to be slightly eccentric.

Little Finger (Sensitivity and Sexuality) and Ring Finger

The length of the little finger is judged in relation to imaginary line (b) drawn through the second phalange of the ring finger (FIG. 92).

Fig. 92 Comparison of the lengths of little fingers

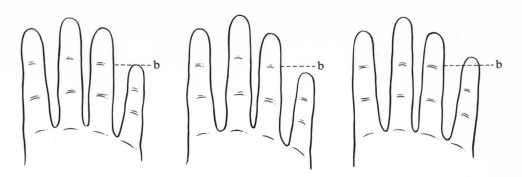

(H) Tip of little finger reaches (b) exactly
The most common type is the one in which the tip of the little finger falls exactly
on line (b). Such people are emotionally stable and, on the average, active. Their
sexual appetites are moderate.

(I) Tip of little finger falls below (b)
Women of this type are not blessed with children and have faint interest in sex.
This little-finger length occurs often in women with retroflexion of the uterus.
   Men with short little fingers take only a cursory interest in sex.

(J) The little finger is very long
People in which the little finger extends well beyond the second phalange of the
ring finger have excellent aesthetic taste and are sexually very attractive. Women
of this kind often have voluptuous eyes and mouths and lovely hips and busts.

Personality Judged on the Basis of Fingernail Shape

Because they have long been recognized as indicators of physical conditions, the
fingernails—their shape and color—play a part in most doctors' diagnoses. The
nail of the index finger—especially its base—is most important in examining
shape. This fingernail is sometimes square (A), sometimes round (B), and sometimes long and slender (C) as shown in Fig. 93. All three types reveal personality
characteristics.

(A) People—often men—with squarish, sturdy-looking nails of this kind are
persevering and extremely positive and vigorous. Women with this kind of finger-

Fig. 93   Kinds of fingernail shapes

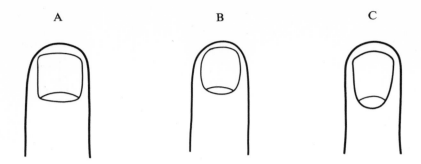

A   B   C

nail loathe the idea of losing and sometimes have stronger personalities than men. This is a highly masculine fingernail shape.

(B)   This type, which is common in both men and women, indicates a warm and accommodating personality. Such people are moderate and get along well with practically anyone. They are, however, weak-willed and tend to follow others' lead.

(C)   People with this kind of nail are often nervous and delicate in personality and tend to be overly sensitive in personal relations, to change their minds often, and to be irritable. Perhaps for this reason they are often slender. But they are sensitive to beauty and have extraordinary powers of imagination.

Relations between Fingernails and Sickness

The following are the most common of the numerous ways in which fingernails reveal physical condition (FIG. 94).

(A)   Half-moons
People in whom the half-moon at the base appears in all five fingers are healthy and have strong metabolism. At about the time of illness, these half-moons can disappear. (Some people lack them congenitally.) People with very large half-moons have great stamina. People in whom the half-moons are missing in little and ring fingers usually are weak in the lower half of the body.

(B)   Vertical striations
Vertical striations in the fingernails are related to the aging process. Very deep, clear striations indicate diabetes.

Fig. 94   Signs of illness occurring in the fingernails

A. Half-moon

B. Vertical
     striations

C. Horizontal
     striations

D. White spots

E. Holes

F. Spoonlike
     deformations

(C)   Horizontal striations
Horizontal grooves sometimes manifest themselves in fingernails after surgery, fever, or injury.

(D)   White spots
White spots occur in the nails after something shocking or delightful has happened. People of long ago were happy to see these spots since they believed they indicated an imminent increase in the size of the person's wardrobe. It is sometimes said that air in the fingernails is their cause.

(E)   Holes
It is said that the fingernails and the hair are closely related. Pinholes occur in the nails as a first sign of falling hair. And victims of spot baldness (alopecia areata) usually have pinholes in their fingernails.

(F)   Deformation
Spoonlike bulges of the fingernails may indicate tuberculosis or internal parasites.

Personality Judged on the Basis of Fingerprints

Immediately conjuring up connections with crime, the fingerprints, which are required for many official documents including driving licenses and, in Japan, alien registration certificates, are not only a highly important means of personal identification, but also significant indicators of much about personality and constitution.

In the United States, at birth a child's footprint and the fingerprint of the mother's index finger are immediately recorded. This of course prevents mistaken identify and parentage of infants in hospitals. In addition, however, it is important in the early detection of congenital sickness.

Estimations of personality on the basis of fingerprints have been made for many years. The Englishman Nöel Jacquin and the Frenchman Henri Mangin are famous researchers in this field.

Three Basic Kinds of Fingerprints

The three basic kinds of fingerprints are whorls (W), which appear as circular whirlpool forms; loops (L), which are wavelike forms oriented toward the thumb or the little finger; and arches (A), which are peaklike forms higher in the center (FIG. 95). These three basic forms may occur in various combinations. All three types, the most common of which is the loop (L) and the least common of which is the arch (A), reveal aspects of individual personality.

Fig. 95   Forms of fingerprints

whorl   loop   arch

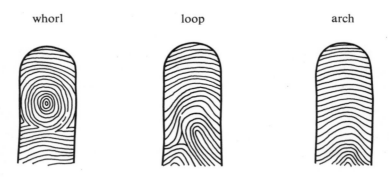

Fingerprints of the Thumb and Index Finger

Since they reveal ego and initiative, the prints of these two fingers are most important in understanding an individual's personality. People in whom the prints of both fingers are (W) hate to lose, are highly positive and active, and refuse to submit to the wills of others. Stubborn, they are bold and undaunted by defeat, no matter how frequent. People in whom the index fingers and thumbs of both hands are (W) are extremely extroverted and adventure-loving.

Index finger only (W)

These people are active and prefer to be always on the move. They have the initiative to put their own ideas into practice and are socially extremely adroit, though they sometimes become irritable and insecure.

Thumb only (W)

On the surface quiet, these people can reveal extreme perseverance. Though they seem to be conformable to the wills of other people, they are actually extremely selfish.

Thumb and index finger (L)

Prudent and cautious, such people always take their surroundings into consideration. Sometimes they become insecure and let chances escape them by thinking about things too much. Though not actually wanting to, they sometimes allow themselves to be dominated.

One of the two (A)

People in which the (A) form occurs in either the thumb or the index finger tend to be emotionally changeable and to demonstrate boldness and resolution on one occasion and weakness and despair on another. In spite of this defect, however, many of them have the genius to improve their fate.

Fingerprints of the Little and Ring Fingers

The prints of these two fingers are related to the individual's powers of original thought, interest in the opposite sex, and artistic talents and therefore provide the key to understanding that person's love expectations and aesthetic creativity.

Both little and ring fingers (W)

People of this kind have extremely high aesthetic ability and creativity and can produce original things impossible for ordinary persons. They are extremely passionate and expressive toward the opposite sex, whom they understand well. People in whom both these fingers in both hands are (W) possess outstanding powers of intuition and an astounding ability to grasp what others are thinking.

Either the little or ring fingers (W)

Such people often demonstrate their powers in expanding special artistic or technical skills and come up with unusual ideas of kinds that ordinary people rarely have. They frequently have a chance for such bright ideas after protracted unpleasantness or trouble in human relations. Though seemingly cool to the opposite sex, they are very gentle and tend to fall in love at first sight. Misfortune and disappointment in love have a stimulating instead of a depressing effect on them.

All fingers (W)

People in which all five fingers are (W) are very sensitive and easily hurt and have outstanding artistic sense. Many of them are chic and have distinctive individual charm. Ironically, however, they frequently are not loved by the people they love or face the passionate admiration of people they find distasteful.

All fingers (L)

People in whom all fingers are (L) are accommodating and are able somehow or another to put up with troublesome situations. They seem weak but actually have a great deal of fortitude and demonstrate fierce will when backed into a corner.

The Palm as a Warning of Illness

Palm Lines and Sickness

Of the six different palm patterns in Fig. 96, (A) is the most standard and the most common. In it, the three major lines are all gently curved; and the initial parts of the Life and Intellect Lines form one clear line. In (B), the beginnings of the Life and Intellect Lines are separate. In (C), which resembles (A), there are many fine lines at the Life Line. In (C), (D), (E), and (F), the beginnings of the Life and Intellect Lines are unclear and the whole palm is covered with a spider web of fine lines.

These patterns reveal differences in the hands of well and sick primary-school children. Of the six, the most healthy is the owner of palm pattern (B). The owner of pattern (D) is a victim of hereditary cardiamorphia, and the owner of pattern (E) was hospitalized for a malignant cardiac ailment. The owner of pattern (F) is a victim of what is called the Down's syndrome, or congenital Mongolism. Though physically strong, the owner of pattern (C) suffers from weak bronchial organs and frequently catches cold.

The initial parts of the Life and Intellect Lines of the palm reveal much about health and about characteristics acquired from the fetal period into infancy. Furthermore, these characteristics most certainly appear in the hands of people hospitalized for tuberculosis, cardiac ailments, and other serious diseases. It is therefore extremely advisable to acquire an accurate understanding of palmistry in order to take suitable precautions while health is still good.

An investigation of people who experienced illness (lasting more than a month) in infancy and those who did not and who did or did not manifest irregularities in the initial part of the Life Line produced the following data.

Fig. 96 Hand forms of six children

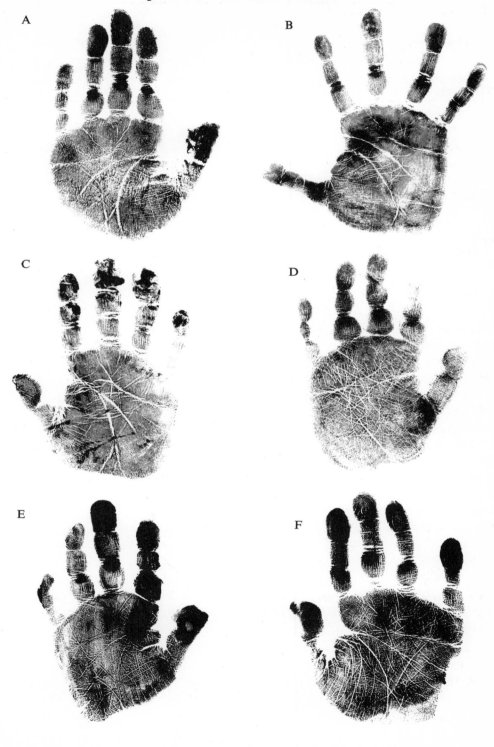

Table 10

	Number of subjects	Were ill in infancy	Were not ill in infancy	Uncertain
Irregularity in the initial part of the Life Line	100	58	31	11
No irregularity in the initial part of the Life Line	100	22	64	14

As the statistics show, the rate of infancy illness is higher in people manifesting irregularity at the start of the Life Line.

The following are the kinds of irregularities occurring in the initial zones of life lines (FIG. 97).

Fig. 97   Abnormalities occurring in the lines or creases of the hands

A. Islands   B. Stars   C. Breaks   D. Disruptions

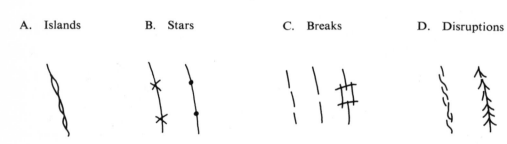

(A)   Islands
Lines intertwine to produce islandlike spaces between themselves. In people with two or more of these irregular formations, the ratio of experience with illness is high. This irregularity is common in victims of infantile paralysis and virtually always occurs in premature infants and infants with congenital deformations.

(B)   Stars
This deformation takes the form of crosses or dots on the Life Line. Though research on it is still insufficient, it seems to manifest itself in cardiac patients.

(C)   Breaks
Breaks in the Life Line, which take the three forms shown in the figure, frequently appear in tubercular people, before the outbreak of the sickness itself. The line becomes whole again when the illness is cured.

(D)   Disruption
Manifest in many people, this deformation has complex, as yet not fully understood, meaning. It occurs in people with abnormal constitutions and allergies.

Hand Shape and Illness

I have shown how the creases of the palm reveal experiences with and tendencies to fall victim to illness. The shape of the hand too is altered by some sicknesses —especially rheumatism and infantile paralysis. Congenital malformations of the hand are often connected with psychological illness. For instance, Fumimaro Urabe, of the University of Kyushu, has shown that the tips of the fingers are especially small in 27.31 percent of mentally retarded children whereas this phenomenon occurs in only 4.82 percent of normal children. The English specialist Charlotte Wolff has pointed out considerable irregularity in hand shapes and palm creases in psychologically ill people. The following are some of the results of her work.

1. *Schizophrenia* (thirteen cases)
   Malformation and shortness of the little and ring fingers in seven cases.
   Irregularity of the index finger in three cases.
2. *Manic-depressive psychosis* (five cases)
   Irregularity of the shape of the thumb in two cases. Irregularity in the Intellect and Fate Lines in all five cases.
3. *Hysteria* (two cases)
   Irregularity in the Emotion Line in both.
4. *Other pathological conditions* (eight cases)
   Irregularities in the thumbs of three cases, irregularities in the little fingers of three cases, irregularities of the index and ring fingers in two cases, and irregularities in the Intellect Line in three cases.

In another report, Charlotte Wolff has said that the majority of 350 mentally retarded children she examined manifested irregularities in the Intellect Line and in the shape of the thumb.

Illness and Changes in the Fingerprints

Noël Jacquin, said to be a student of Cheiro,* is responsible for applying the study of fingerprints, now widely used as a means of legally establishing identity, to judgment of personality and illness on the basis of palmistry. Many scholars have shown interest in Jacquin's research into changes in fingerprints and their relation to illness. Outstanding among other research workers in this field is Harold Cummins, of the Department of Medicine of Tulane University, and R. Churille of Scotland Yard, who, in cooperation with medical specialists, showed that signs of illness generally appear in the fingerprints of the left hand, although work on

---

* Cheiro, a famous Irish seer born in 1866. His book *Language of the Hand* is considered an origin of modern palmistry.

which illnesses affect the fingerprints is still insufficient. Some American scholars have shown that continuous exposure to a minute amount of x-ray radiation causes creases to develop in chimpanzee fingerprints, the shape of which is disturbed. Both disorders are cleared up in a few weeks after exposure to radiation is terminated.

In one of his reports, R. Churille said that doctors who had been subjected to radiation damage in the left hand manifested broken shapes in the fingerprints of the right hand. In other words, changes in the fingertips indicate a total body change and not merely a change in the fingertips themselves. This is true because of connections between the nervous system and the biochemical tendency of the papillary layer constituting the fingerprints. This is why serious disorders in the nervous tissues and other cellular tissues reveal themselves in alterations in the highly sensitive fingerprints. In general, these changes take the form of creases that destroy the pattern of the print (FIG. 98). Investigation of these irregularities reveals the part of the body that is ill. Various sicknesses, including cancer, infantile paralysis, and rheumatism, affect the fingerprints.

Fig. 98 Abnormalities in the fingerprints

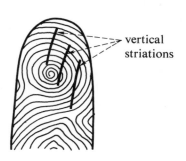

vertical striations

Illness and the Fingernails

Usually, in healthy people, whitish half-moons occur at the bases of all fingernails, whereas this is not the case in people who are unwell and whose blood is of a poor color. In 1963, Professor Theodore Berry, of the Department of Medicine of the University of Pennsylvania, as a result of a series of studies on the relation between the hands and illness, published a book called *The Hand as a Mirror of Systemic Diseases*, in which he said that the half-moons and horizontal creases in the fingernails as well as changes in the color and creases of the palm are often expressions of illness. Like the fingerprints, the nails are an excellent barometer of overall bodily condition. Excess nervous strain, lack of sleep, and overfatigue cause the half-moons to disappear entirely and create vertical creases in the nails.

Illness as Revealed in the Hand

Although the full reasons are not understood, probably because of connections with the endocrine system, the hands represent a linkage of all the bodily functions. Exerting an influence on the whole body, through changes in their shapes, the hands reflect illness, alterations in condition, and gains and losses of weight. The deformation rheumatism causes in the hand is a classical example of this. Some kinds of cerebral disorders, which affect, of course, the brain, account for deformation of the hands too. The following case is an interesting indication of the way the hands affect the whole body. A person caught his right middle finger in a door jamb; and after a while, its tip bent. After the passage of some more time, the tip of the left middle finger 'too bent.

The ancient philosopher Hippocrates noticed that the nails and fingers of tubercular people change in characteristic ways; still today, the medical profession refers to this phenomenon as Hippocratic nails.

The extent to which gout and rheumatism have progressed can be judged from such changes in the fingers as alterations in the joints. In instances of Raynaud's disease, the hands turn white or bluish. Connections with the endocrine system mean that irritability or other nervous disorders change the shape of the hand and the color of its skin. For instance, manic-depressives usually have weak, pale-bluish, slender hands. The hands of people suffering from schizophrenia are slender and yellowish in cast.

Research in this field has been vigorous in many parts of the world, especially since the 1950s. The French physician and palmist Henri Mangin, who evolved the term *medical palmistry*, has done much research analyzing the relation between the hands and illness. In addition, the English researcher Noël Jacquin has studied the connection between the hands and the ailments of cancer, tuberculosis, and rheumatism patients. The famous French spiritualist researcher Baracool, has investigated relations between the various parts of the body and the hand in terms of what is called *radiesthesia*. In addition, in England and America, a great deal of study has been devoted to the configuration of the hand in connection with genetic research and psychological sickness. And, in Japan, at the cardiac laboratory of the Tokyo Woman's University, Professor Atsuyoshi Takao has investigated the hand in connection with cardiamorphia.

Health Diagnosis and the Hand

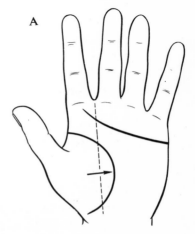

Fig. 99 *Illness and palmar creases*

Investigation of changes in the parts of the hands and irregularities in palmar creases makes possible a degree of prognosis about constitution and sickness, as many medical specialists in the West have already shown. Since for more detailed diagnoses sophisticated medical knowledge is essential, I will introduce only a few easy methods (FIG. 99). It must be remembered that these diagnoses are only partial. Consultation with a physician is required for final analysis.

(A) People who tend to live long
The creases are deep and clear. The Life Line is long, and the Emotion Line extends straight to the base of the index finger.

B

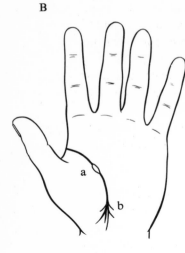

(B)   People who tend to have weak digestions
In people in whom, the Life Line is islandlike (a) and the end
is split (b), the stomach is upset whenever their way of life
becomes even slightly irregular. They should avoid alcohol
and heavy eating and should always eat breakfast.

(C)   People prone to cancer
Cancer and apoplexy are among the two most dreaded and
deadly diseases afflicting humanity today. Though young
people do not often fall victim to apoplexy, cancer, in such
forms as leukemia, strikes people of all age groups. People
in whom the islandlike crease seen in (a) are numerous or in
whom X-shaped configurations (b) are numerous near the
Life Line should be cautious and consult a physician.

C

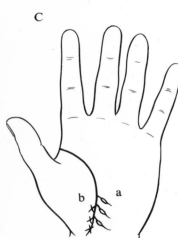

(D)   People prone to bronchial illness
People in whom, instead of forming a straight line, the beginning of the Intellect Line is a chainlike configuration, tend to
have weak bronchia and respiratory organs and catch cold
and tire easily. When the situation advances further, islandlike
configurations appear above the Life Line.

(E)   People prone to cardiac illnesses
Frequently, people in whom there is a black spot (a) in the
center of the Emotion Line have some kind of cardiac irregularity and suddenly fall victim to fatal sickness. People
in whom the Emotion Line is broken as in (b) may have
a hereditary heart ailment.

D

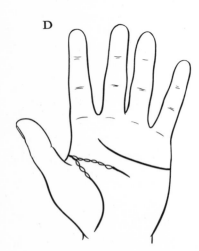

E

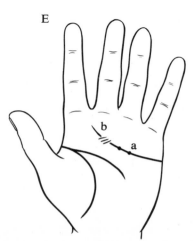

F

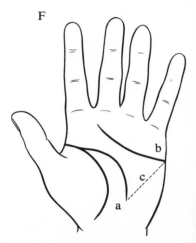

(F)   People prone to neuroses

The present, with its brutal cities, complexities, lack of warm contact, and difficulties in human relations, is an age in which many people tend to be neurotic. People in whom the terminal point of the Intellect Line (a) and the starting point of the Emotion Line (b) are separated become neurotic easily. In people of sounder mental health, the distance (c) between (a) and (b) is shorter.

Using the Configuration of the Hand to Discover Sickness

As I have already shown in discussing the disorders that occur during the fetal period, irregularities in the configuration of the hand reveal physical and psychological faults in infants. The following discussion deals with how to use the configuration of the hand to discover these disorders.

The hand in FIG. 100-A is of an infant with a hereditary organic disorder. Although in all other outward respects perfectly normal, the child reveals this illness through malformation of the hand pattern. In pattern (A), which is that of an infant with congenital organ malformation, the Intellect Line is connected midway with the Emotion Line. Recent investigations have shown that many infants with hands like (B), similar to the so-called *masukake* pattern in that the Intellect Line runs straight across the palm without descending toward the wrist, suffer from congenital organic malformations. This palm pattern was discovered by a group of doctors from Sydney, who named it the Sydney Line. An important clue in the detection of congenital irregularities and organic malformations, this hand pattern occurred in as much as 38 percent of a group of children suffering from leukemia and other disorders.

In addition to the palm pattern itself, the palm print of small fingerprintlike lines in the hand can be a sign of congenital malformation. According to the American doctor Harold Cummins and his associates, leading authorities in research in this field, in infants with congenital malformation, the T-shaped pattern, at the base of the wrist, usually occurring singly in normal children, is often double and positioned slightly higher than in healthy infants (C).

Reliable judgments on the basis of these three palm patterns require sophisticated medical knowledge and long experience. It is dangerous for uninformed laymen to attempt them. For

Fig. 100   Signs of illness in the palmar creases of children's hands

A

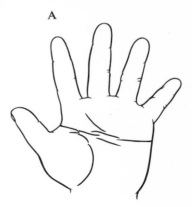

B

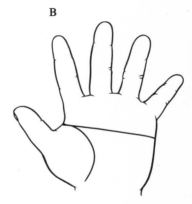

C

normal

Fig. 101   Illness and children's Life Lines

A

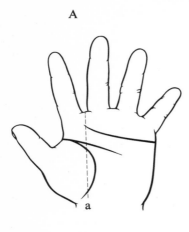

B

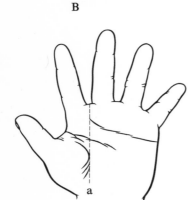

the purposes of this book, however, an awareness of these palm patterns and palm prints can be medically useful in the discovery and treatment of congenital malformations.

Caution should be exerted in dealing with infants whose palms are covered with a virtual spider web of fine creases obscuring the Life and Intellect Lines since they are often victims of endocrine disorders and tend to catch asthma and eczema easily.

In normal, healthy developing infants, the Life Line is deep, clear, and long; and, aside from the three basic lines, there are few other small creases in the palm. In a poorly developed infant, however, the Life Line stops inside an imaginary line (a) drawn between the closed index and middle fingers and extended across the palm (FIG. 101-B). The end of the line is often faint or broken into several creases. Instead of forming a single line as in (A), the initial parts of the Life and Intellect Lines are characteristically broken as in (B). The entire palm is covered with creases and looks irregular.

The German doctor W. Debrunner examined the palms of healthy and abnormal newborn infants and compiled the classifications and occurrence percentages shown in TABLE 11.

Table 11

	Normal infants	Abnormal infants
Numerous creases in the hypothenar region only	53%	14%
Numerous creases in the thenar region only	2%	0
Numerous creases all over the hand	45%	86%

In the cases of healthy infants, patterns of the type shown in FIG. 102-A, in which creases are numerous only on the hypothenar, or patterns like the one in FIG. 102-B, in which they are numerous only in the vicinity of the thenar, occurred. As infants of the type with pattern (A) grow older, the creases in the hypothenar region tend to decrease. Those with the (B) pattern are sometimes slightly frail; but, with proper nourishment in a good environment, the numbers of lines decrease. Infants with many lines in the vicinities of both the thenar and the hypothenar are the ones that cause most trouble. In premature or stillborn infants, this palm pattern is frequent.

Fig. 102 *Innumerable creases appearing on the hypothenar and thenar*

A

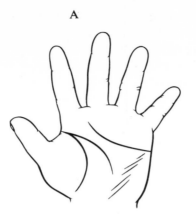

B

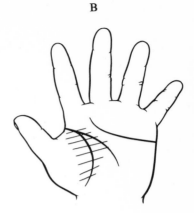

Old books on palmistry said that children with these palm patterns are fated to die early. And perhaps, in former times, when conditions were different and infant mortality was high, this prediction was reasonable. Today, however, with improved modern medicine and a higher standard of living, infants with broken Life Lines and numerous other creases in the palm can be safely raised to adulthood; and there is no need for parents to be pessimistic if their children manifest this kind of palm pattern. Older systems of palmistry require revisions on a number of points of this kind.

Now I shall turn to the use of the palm pattern in detecting psychological disorders. FIG. 103 shows the palm pattern of a normal infant and that of a congenitally retarded infant afflicted with Down's syndrome (Mongolism). The two major differences in them are related to the flow of lines and the length of the little finger. In the normal infant, the three basic lines curve gently and naturally. In the Mongoloid child's palm, on the other hand, the Intellect and Emotion Lines overlap and cross the palm on the horizontal. As a comparison of their lengths shows, a very short little finger is one of the most salient signs of Down's syndrome. In some instances there is only one joint crease on the little finger instead of the normal two. And suspicion of Down's syndrome is even stronger when, as in this case, the thumb is malformed or abnormally close to the wrist. The results of extensive research on the differences in the hands of normal and Mongoloid children by the Austria-born specialist Charlotte Wolff have come in for great note in the scholarly field of psychology. If the little finger is short with swollen joints and a bend in the direction of the ring finger, even when no signs of

Fig. 103 *Hands of a normal infant and an infant suffering from Down's syndrome*

A

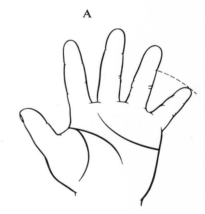

B

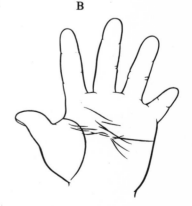

Down's syndrome are apparent, the infant's physical and mental development should be carefully monitored for any indications of abnormality.

In *The Hand as a Mirror of Systemic Diseases*, Dr. Theodore Berry of the University of Pennsylvania has said that an unusually long little finger is frequent in schizophrenics. In either case, the length of the little finger, which is said to be related to the thyroid gland and hence to metabolism, is an important indication of sound or abnormal development and is therefore significant in this connection and in relation to the infant's future. Nonetheless, parents should not worry if their children manifest hand patterns of these kinds, since modern medicine is discovering ways of overcoming the difficulties. Furthermore, as shall be discussed in detail later, when the infant's condition changes owing to environment conditions, these hand patterns too alter.

Some people may doubt that signs of future unhappiness can manifest themselves in a child's palm, but I have already indicated that such is the case. First, to detect signs of unhappiness, it is essential to examine the palm for abnormal lines of the kind shown in FIG. 104. Under ordinary circum-

Fig. 104   Kinds of abnormalities appearing in palmar creases

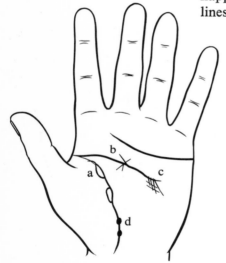

Fig. 105   Relations between the hand and the various parts and systems of the human body

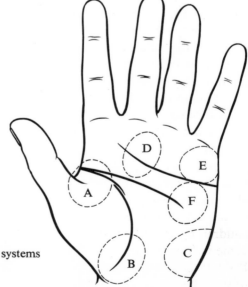

Mainly part A—respiratory system
Mainly part B—alimentary system
Mainly part C—liver system
Mainly part D—cardiac and vascular systems
Mainly part E—nervous system
Mainly part F—lower body

stances, palmar lines are single; but, when certain special conditions are present, variations may occur.

(1) *Oval, islandlike lines* (a).   These may occur in other places but are most frequent in the Life, Emotion, and Intellect Lines.

(2) *Crossmarks* (b).   These occur in the center of the palm or in the vicinities of the three basic lines.

(3) *Fine grill patterns* (c).   These occur at the bases of the index or little fingers or on the upper surface of the thenar.

(4) *Spots* (d).   Blackish spots arranged in lines.

In making examinations, first remember the locations of abnormal lines of these kinds, which, depending on the places where they occur, can be signs of illness, indications of various psychological handicaps, or harbingers of trouble in life.

Although islandlike formations occur in infants with physical deformations or Down's syndrome and in the hereditarily retarded children, they are seen in normal infants too. Charlotte Wolff's investigations have produced the following ratios of occurrence frequency.

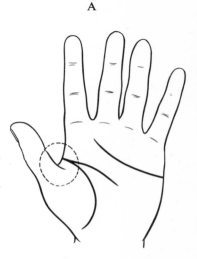

Fig. 106   Abnormalities in the Life Line

A

Table 12

	Islandlike forms in the Intellect Line	Islandlike forms in the Emotion Line
Normal people	20%	22%
Idiots	30%	74%
Mentally retarded people	26.1%	39.1%

In addition to these strong connections with abnormalities, the pattern of the hand is, as has been said, connected with the discovery of illness. In dealing with children under investigation, variations in the numbers of lines and creases in the palm and in the shape and color of the fingernails should be examined carefully. Signs of irregularity in the parts of the body appear in the parts of the hand as shown in FIG. 105. Judging health on the basis of the hand and palm requires a very high level of medical knowledge. It is set forth in detail in the book *The Hand as a Mirror of Systemic Diseases* by Dr. Theodore Berry of the University of Pennsylvania. Here, however, I shall limit myself to a few simple applications of the kind that can be made in daily life.

Each year the number of children suffering from infantile asthma increases. In normal, healthy children, the Life Line is a clear line (FIG. 106-A). In children with weak bronchial

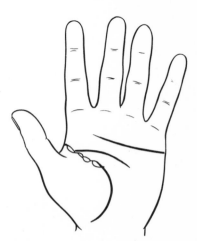

B

C

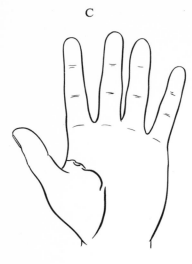

Fig. 107

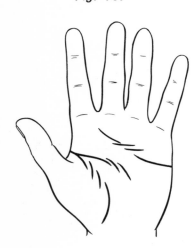

tubes, however, it assumes a chainlike, indistinct configuration like the one in (B). As the situation worsens, the Life Line assumes the islandlike configuration or, at the worst, breaks as in (C). In children suffering from infantile tuberculosis, the Life Line is invariably broken. But there is no serious cause to worry because the Life Line is short. Many children demonstrate short or doubled Life Lines that return to normal as the pathological condition causing them is corrected.

People in which the three basic lines are not clear, as in FIG. 107, but irregular tend to tire easily. They often lack half-moons, or lunulae, at the bases of their fingernails. Short-term illnesses often cause changes in the fingernails. For instance, horizontal grooves or steplike configurations occur in the upper part of the fingernails about a month or two after a sickness or in the lower parts of the nails when body condition has been abnormal more recently. In cases of fairly advanced or chronic sickness, the nails tend to mound or become roundish in contour.

Although research into the topic is too young to have solved all problems, the following abnormalities in the patterning of the palm and other aspects of the hands in relation to hereditary organic malformation and congenital mental retardation may be cited.

1. Abnormalities in the Intellect and Emotion Lines
2. Abnormalities in the fingerprints
3. Abnormalities in the palm prints

According to research by an American doctor named Fred Rosener, abnormal palm patterns occurred in only 5 or 6 percent of healthy people; whereas 41.2 percent of 154 people afflicted with Down's syndrome demonstrated this pattern. The same pattern occurred in 33.3 percent of a group of patients of phenylketonuria, and was more than 6 times more common in people with some kind of hereditary abnormality than in normal people.

The Sydney Line is said to be frequent in patients of infantile leukemia. Dr. F. W. Miller and his group at Sydney University discovered the FIII and Sydney patterns in eighteen out of twenty-five cases of leukemia, three of whom died during the investigation.

Palm patterns too differ in healthy and hereditarily ill people, especially in connection with the location of the

T-shaped pattern on the palm near the wrist (FIG. 108).
Measuring its position is done by means of what is called the
ATD angle, which is the angle near the wrist formed by
joining the T-shaped figures at the bases of the index and little
fingers with the T-shaped figure near the wrist by means of
two lines. In 91.5 percent of all healthy individuals, this angle
is less than 57 degrees. In people with congenital abnormalities, it is higher than 57 degrees in 65 percent of all cases.

In one of his research reports, L. S. Penrose, a noted authority on the subject, has said that the numbers of grooves
in the whorls of fingerprints vary between healthy people and
people with some abnormality. For instance, in the fingerprint of the thumb of an ordinary woman, there are roughly
ten grooves (FIG. 109). But this number can increase to thirteen or decrease to about eight as a result of abnormalities
altering the numerical combination of the sex chromosomes,
which are strongly influenced by heredity.

In conclusion, it should be pointed out that accidents and
psychological shock as well as illness can cause alterations
in the lines of the palm pattern.

Fig. 108   The ATD Angle

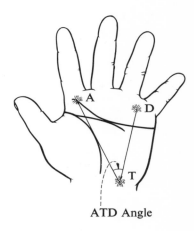

ATD Angle

Fig. 109   Grooves in fingerprints

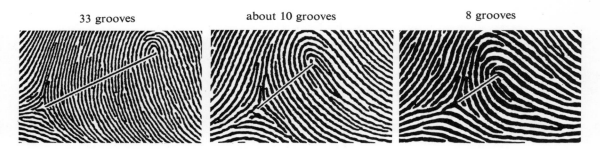

33 grooves   about 10 grooves   8 grooves

A Person's Past Revealed in the Palm

Because of the prominence of manual work and the need to use the hands to
manipulate tools, a person's occupation is most clearly revealed by his hands. In
his *La Main et l'Esprit*, Jean Brun says that, to one extent or another, an individual's past life is engraved on his hand, as are his social position and occupational activities. Many years of manual labor alter the shape of the hands in

characteristic ways and are linked with the way the brain and the hands are connected and with psychological life. The hands of a pianist, a seamstress, and a shiatsu practitioner are all modified in different ways, though all three occupations involve use of the fingertips. The shapes of hands of people who do intellectual work and those who do physical work are different, and the hands of a person who does no work at all are different from those of these two types.

People like thinkers and researchers, whose work, while entailing little physical exertion, makes great demands on the mind have slender fingers; and their entire hands are covered with fine lines. Their hands look frail; and, because of the great mental stress they experience, their fingers are always bent. The skin of their palms is soft, and they have numerous creases at the bases of their thumbs.

The ends of the fingers of people whose work is physical are thick. The fingers themselves are short; and the palms have a massive, sturdy look and few wrinkles. The three fundamental lines are deeply etched. Owing to the strenuous physical nature of their work, their nails are often deformed and broken. Often they have calluses on their palms and wounds on the backs of their hands.

People who depend on others and do neither mental nor physical labor, have lovely, soft, white hands that are balanced, slender, and free of deformations.

Calluses and alterations of shape are well-known results of extended manual labor. For instance, writers who hold pencils or pens tightly in their hands frequently develop calluses on the inner side of the middle finger. Carpenters, electricians, or other people who constantly use screwdrivers or gimlets develop them on the palms at the base of the thumb and near the index finger. Irons or plasterers' trowels make calluses on the parts of the hand with which they come into contact. People who do a great deal of hammering or hoeing usually have calluses at the bases of the four fingers.

Masseurs and practitioners of shiatsu, who employ frequent pushing motions with their fingers have thick fingertips; and the fingers—especially the thumbs—with which they exert pressure tend to be heavy.

Since it is the most difficult of the digits to use, the little finger rarely reveals deformations, though it is crooked in people, like beauticians and barbers, whose work calls for frequent use of scissors.

The use of water or chemicals and other staining substances leaves its traces on the hands. The yellowed fingers of heavy smokers is one example, as are discolored hands of pharmacists or dyers. Launderers—in Japan manufacturers of tofu or bean curd too—must keep their hands in water a great deal of the time with the result that their skin turns whitish and the numbers of creases decrease, greatly simplifying palm patterns.

Charlotte Wolff has called attention to the effects of musical and artistic occupations on the shapes of hands and fingers. For instance, as she points out, a pianist's hands are usually large and supple and have broad fingertips. Repeated practice of the same motions has a conspicuously broadening effect on the finger ends of people who play string instruments. Sculptors characteristically have highly developed; short, strong, regular fingers with broad tips; and very simple line patterns.

Sports too affect the shapes of hands and fingers, as is most vividly seen in the golfers' and baseball players' calluses and manual deformations. Pitchers who specialize in trick balls often reveal index fingers that have grown as long as their middle fingers (some men with index and middle fingers congenitally the same length use this trait to good advantage in pitching). Bowlers often have deformed thumbs and broken nails and tend to develop calluses or wounds easily on their thumb tips. Practitioners of the Japanese martial art of kendo fencing frequently have deformed or broken fingernails, which they tend to cut very short.

Work-related Fortune

Finding the age division of the Fate Line, the vertical line down the center of the palm from the base of the middle finger to the wrist, is done as shown in FIG. 110. Though the Fate Line is unclear in some people, a close examination of the pertinent age division on it is necessary. For example, in the palm shown in the figure, the place where the Intellect Line and the Fate Line intersect occurs at the age division for age thirty-three.

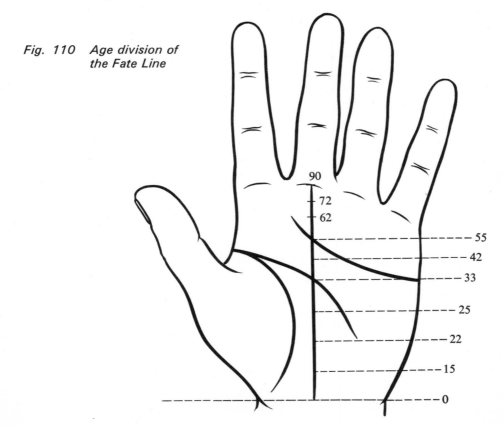

Fig. 110   Age division of the Fate Line

Fig. 111   The occupationally unstable type

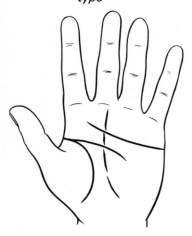

1.   The occupationally unstable type

The Fate Line is referred to as the Social Line since it indicates the individual's attitude toward life and work. In the pattern in Fig. 111, the line is either broken or totally missing. An absence of a Fate Line after the age of twenty indicates serious occupational instability, no clear goals for the future, high dreams unaccompanied by the ability to make them come true, and a tendency to dreaminess.

2.   The winner type

People who have a long, clear Fate Line from the base of the middle finger to the wrist are of two types (Fig. 112). Either, since childhood, they have lived blessed lives in which they have realized all their wishes, or they are the kind of people who have clear goals and see anything they undertake through to completion.

Fig. 112   The winner type

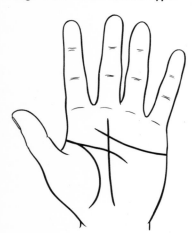

3.   The type that can expect a change in fortune

In this type, which is interpreted similarly in both ancient Indian and ancient Western palmistry, numerous star or cross creases appear on the Fate Line (Fig. 113). They are interpreted to be either lucky or unlucky, but mean a change. For instance a person who has been experiencing a run of bad luck at home and on the job, can hope for a change for the better. But, in many instances, a person whose fortune heretofore has been good must be prepared for a change for the worse.

Fig. 114   The type that succeeds through the help of others

Fig. 113   The type that can expect a change in fortune

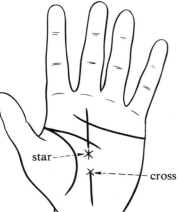

star- - - -*

X - - - - - cross

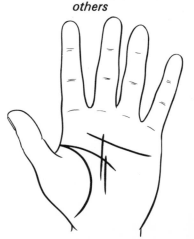

4. The type that succeeds through the help of others
When a small line running parallel to the Fate Line appears,
an assistant will turn up on the job to help the individual
succeed in undertakings in which he has hitherto failed
(FIG. 114). Before attempting things on their own, people
with this pattern will find that their efforts are more effective
if they first discuss the situation with seniors and explain
whatever is troubling them.

5. The type that is easily influenced in private life
Intersections in the Fate Line indicate changes in private life
at the ages corresponding to their locations on the palm. In
general, the crease running from the base of the thumb to the
Fate Line is very significant (FIG. 115). If it is long and deep,
it indicates profound influence on private life. A long clear
line like this is called the Obstruction Line, or the Hargate
Line, after the American novelist J. B. Hargate, who was
very interested in it. People in which it is accompanied by
numerous radiant lines leading from the thumb tend to be
high-strung and to suffer from complexes in connection with
their own private lives and with work as well.

Work Rhythm

Using the Fate Line, it is possible to judge much about the
rhythm and condition of a person's work. To do this, it is
necessary to refer to figures and to examine the Fate Line and
the various creases and lines appearing on it.

Change in Fortune

A) I have already discussed the cross and star lines appearing on the Fate Line (FIG. 116-A) and, in both Indian and
Western palmistry, interpreted to mean a change, for better
or worse, in fate. If these cross and star creases appear in
both hands, it is wise to be cautious in connection with
fortune for a year or two. (Creases of these kinds appeared
in the hand of the famous nineteenth-century French actress
Sarah Bernhardt.) People who are twenty-three (that is, not
in the twenty-third year but have actually been alive twenty-
three full years); thirty-two, forty-one, fifty, or fifty-nine
should be prepared for a worsening in their fortune if these

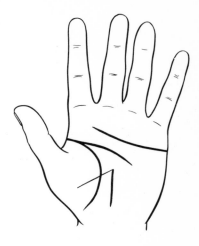

*Fig. 115   The type that
is easily influenced
in private life*

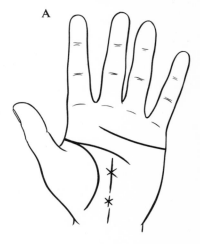

*Fig. 116   Indications ap-
pearing in the
Fate Line of a
change in fortune*

B

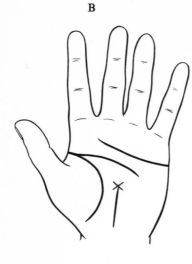

C

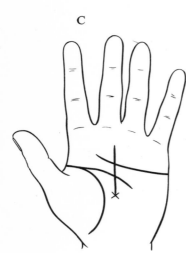

stars appear and if they change jobs or start a different kind of work. On the other hand, people who are nineteen, twenty-one, twenty-eight, thirty, thirty-seven, or thirty-nine and who have experienced no marked success or good fortune in the past may hope for fine opportunities or the appearance of someone to help and cooperate with them.

B) A pattern like (B) in FIG. 116, in which the cross appears at the termination of the Fate Line, is characteristic of great change. Individuals in which it occurs at a location corresponding to current age should alter plans to begin new work or initiate deliberate expansions of any kind. It is possible that sudden changes in exterior circumstances could cause difficulty bringing about a change in work that has heretofore gone smoothly. Special caution is warranted in connection with new work, contracts, or the borrowing or lending of money since grave reversals are possible.

C) People in whom the cross or star is at the beginning of the Fate Line (FIG. 116-C) and who have succeeded in nothing they have undertaken may look to discover suddenly support from those around them or the appearance of a strong ally. Often this takes the form of unexpected assistance from old schoolmates or class seniors whom one happens to meet at a reunion. Or an old friend from whom there has been no correspondence for a long time may suddenly get in touch and bring about a change of fortune. A change for the better in luck is likely in people with this kind of Fate Line who are twenty-five, twenty-nine, thirty-four, thirty-nine, forty-eight, or fifty-seven years old.

Succeeding with Others' Help

The short line parallel to the Fate Line (FIG. 117) indicates the appearance of a good advisor or helper whose assistance will make possible success for a person who, heretofore, has not succeeded. Should a person whose influence is adverse or harmful appear, this short parallel line disappears.

The proper reading of the Fate Line and the creases around it is extremely difficult and is one of the things that makes apparently simple palmistry much harder than it seems. Politicians and businessmen who are blessed with good staffs of workers and helpers virtually always have good Fate Lines and parallel creases. In interpreting them, it is important to ascertain the relation between these lines and the location on the palm corresponding to the person's full age. This sometimes makes it possible to predict a change for the better in a career that has been lackluster so far if the parallel line appears at a position slightly above the location corresponding to current age. But, as is often said, fate is made, not granted; and effort can alter both the Fate Line and this parallel crease.

Timing Success

In this investigation, for people under thirty-three years of age, it is necessary to examine the (A) location slightly below the Intellect Line (FIG. 118). For people thirty-four or older, it is necessary to examine the (B) location slightly above the Intellect Line.

1) Persons in whom the Fate Line is single and clear have an excellent chance of success in the next two or three years and should continue in their present occupation and occupational locations.

2) Persons with a double Fate Line will meet another person who will cooperate with them and will understand their abilities. They should strive for the best and closest possible relations with seniors and superiors.

3) A star crease in position (A) or (B) means an imminent, unanticipated change for the better, a change that is connected with success. The appearance of a branch (a) from the Life Line means that a trip abroad, a change of job, a change in residence, or a business trip can exert a positive influence.

4) The efforts and hard work of people whose Fate Line arises from their Life Line are likely to find recognition in the form of assignment to a position of responsibility.

5) People in whom the Fate Line is divided in two find their chances for success in changing their work, starting something new, altering their policies, or switching to a different line of endeavor.

6) People with Fate Lines broken in a number of places find success only after having experienced numerous hardships and slumps. Their work undergoes cycles and changes about once in three years.

7) A horizontal line crossing the Fate Line often means a failure or difficulty in connection with work. Frequently people with this pattern are irritable and upset because others fail to understand their sincere efforts.

8) People with islandlike creases on their Fate Lines often undergo a great deal of hardship. But rushing only makes

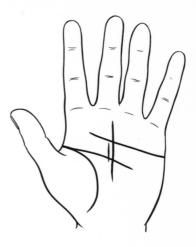

Fig. 117 Short line parallel with the Fate Line

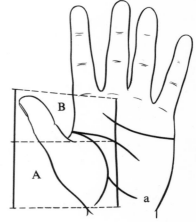

Fig. 118 Using the Fate line to time success

matters worse. They should plan far ahead and look for the fulfillment of their dreams in three or five years' time.

9)   Square creases on the Fate Line mean that it is possible to overcome any trouble or suffering and to find wonderful good fortune.

10)   A vertical line arising from the base of the ring finger and running beside the Fate Line indicates excellent fortune and the chance to put one's talents to optimum use. This pattern often appears in people who independently initiate their own businesses. It must be remembered, however, that a change in ways of thinking can alter the nature of the palm pattern and that, to an extent, effort too can change it.

Personality Revealed in the Palm

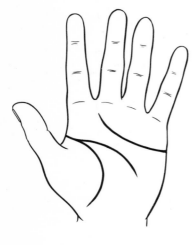

Fig. 119   The steady, well-liked type

The steady, well-liked type
People in whom the Emotion Line curves gently and lies between the index and middle fingers dislike adventure and are serious (FIG. 119). Those with this standard and very common pattern have bright personalities and are liked and trusted by their associates. They get along well with people. White-collar workers of this type proceed step by step, with unostentatious effort, to expand their fortune by making the best use of their abilities and qualifications. When the initial parts of the Life and Intellect Lines overlap, such people are conformable and docile and extremely good at personal relations. They often lack decisiveness and deliberateness. They frequently work for first-class business firms or in offices or banks. In love affairs, they suddenly become introspective and miss opportunities. Husbands of this type dote on their children and are devoted to their homes. Such people lead satisfied lives if they share educational backgrounds or other interests with their spouses.

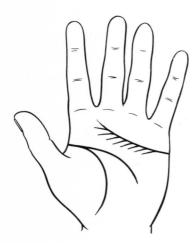

Fig. 120   The type that tries to please everybody

The type that tries to please everybody
The presence of many downward branching lines beside the Emotion Line indicates a person who is self-sacrificing and very careful of the needs of others (FIG. 120). Such people often suffer from worrying too much over small matters. Because they care about what others think of them, they allow themselves to be guided by the opinions of their associates and, trying to please everyone, are often unexpectedly mis-

understood. They are easily betrayed. Clumsy at expressing themselves to others, they frequently love unrequitedly. This tendency is notably strong in people whose Intellect Line is long toward the wrist. Women of this type are gentle wives and homemakers.

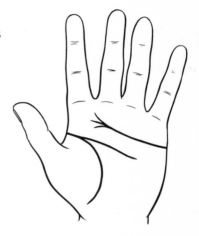

Fig. 121   The sympathetic and helpful type

The sympathetic and helpful type

People with a triple forking of the end of the Emotion Line are kind, tender, and loving but are able to adjust their actions to their surroundings with a certain cool calm (FIG. 121). They strive to satisfy their partners both physically and psychologically. Ironically, however, they are often unwelcome to the people they like and sought by people they dislike. They are loved by juniors and seniors alike because of their inability to stand by silent when others are in trouble. Their fault is a tendency to do too much for people. They are often unhappy in love and, because of disappointment with the opposite sex, sometimes manifest homosexual tendencies.

The stable, enduring type

A double Emotion Line with a short crease below the base of the middle finger and a longer one extending to the base of the little finger indicates a person of strong, persevering willpower (FIG. 122). With leadership abilities and decisiveness, such a person faithfully carries out any assigned task and can make the best use of fortune by being forward and deliberate in personal relations. Men with this pattern tend to like sports. They drink a great deal and have many friends on the job. Though outwardly reticent, they are often boldly passionate. Whereas sometimes unfortunate in love because of the chilly appearance produced by their inability to reveal their true feelings, once in love, they become blindly passionate in a way that draws their partner into the same mood. They tend to become slightly selfish after marriage but lead very cautious lives. Women with this pattern tend to be very strong and to do anything they undertake better than average. Although they become more ordinary as they grow older, they usually develop stable personal relations.

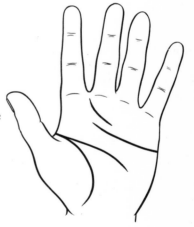

Fig. 122   The stable, enduring type

The troublesome and moody type

An Emotion Line broken in a number of places indicates a highly sensitive, passionate personality (FIG. 123). When they are interested in something, people of this type demonstrate great fervor but tend to become bored quickly. They

Fig. 123   The troublesome and moody type

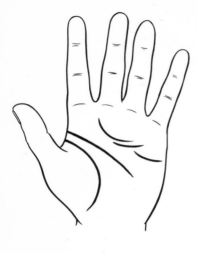

succeed if given the chance to manifest their aesthetic sense or to engage in artistic work. Frequent in women, in men the pattern indicates a nervous personality quick to become absorbed in something and ready to show interest in the beautiful and the novel. Pursuers of dreams, such people have good ideas but lack the ability to put them into practice. They have violent likes and dislikes in human beings, sometimes refusing to speak to people they consider offensive. In bursts of anger they find it difficult to control themselves. It is important for them to have friends to advise them since they easily lose the mental breadth to judge other people objectively. Moody, they change their preferences in members of the opposite sex easily and are often strongly influenced by first impression, external appearance, and style. They cause rifts among their associates because of the unstable way they become very enthusiastic and then suddenly cool off. Preferring romantic to arranged marriages, they have difficulty finding a partner to their liking. People of this pattern in whom the initial parts of the Life and Intellect Lines are separated are often sexually attractive but very much prone to difficulty in finding a suitable partner. They mature quickly and are confident of their faces and figures. In marriage, they tend to cool quickly and often change in their affections. Generally they marry either very early or very late, and the duration between meeting and marriage can be short. Men with this pattern tend to be slightly selfish, overbearing husbands. Women tend to be attractive to considerably older men. During the dating period, people of this type are gentle and skillful at pleasing their partners.

Fig. 124   The reliable leader type

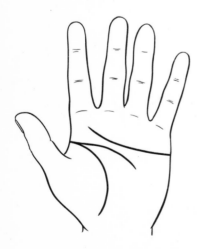

The reliable leader type

An Emotion Line extending far toward the base of the index finger indicates strong will and an ability to consider and deal with things in a cool-headed way (FIG. 124). People with this pattern can always be leaders in any occupation and tend to center their lives on their work, in which they usually succeed. Their reliability makes them trusted by their associates. They can manifest their abilities still more by aquiring specific technical skills and qualifications. They are often mistakenly criticized for coolness because of their hesitancy to express their emotions.

They are proud and attracted by people of high intellectual ability. They have many friends; but, owing to an inability to be sweet and affectionate, marriage presents a problem.

They frequently make arranged marriages or marry people
who were originally only friends, and the period of courtship
tends to be long. But, once in love, they can become astonish-
ingly bold and passionate in actions. Even after marriage,
work occupies the place of central importance in their lives.
Husbands of this type, while domineering and slightly selfish,
are totally reliable. Women of this type like to win and have
the initiative to qualify themselves in various fields of endeavor. Once married, however, they become their husband's
helpmates. Often they find greater satisfaction in married life
than in the period of romantic love and courtship. People of
this type are often so wrapped up in their work that they do
not marry till late.

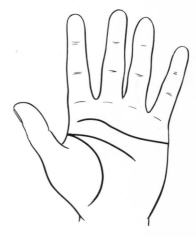

*Fig. 125   The boss who
looks out for
people*

The boss who looks out for people

People in whom the end of the Emotion Line curves downward in the direction of the thumb are demonstrative, have
high ideals, and are dissatisfied with the ordinary (FIG. 125).
They have the characteristics needed for a boss. Outstanding
leaders who look out for the welfare of their people, they
sometimes make enemies because of the stubborn way in
which they push through things they think are good. They
tend to display fits of anger when things displease them and
are too self-centered to worry about pleasing others. Always
concentrating on work, they devote themselves to it completely in the hope of seizing opportunities. Undaunted by
a failure or two, they often succeed after the age of thirty.
Though they rarely stick to one occupation, they are frequently engaged in business or technical fields. Often they
are bachelors or do not marry till late. Shy in love, they miss
their chances by adopting a disconcertingly chilly attitude
toward members of the opposite sex. Frequently they find
good partners in arranged marriages. It is important for
them to remember to smile. Husbands tend to rule with
a strong hand and frequently demonstrate great passion after
marriage.

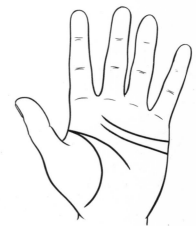

*Fig. 126   The tolerant,
persevering type*

The tolerant, persevering type

A double Emotion Line—one beside the other—indicates
great perseverance and the strength to control one's own
emotions and desires (FIG. 126). Such people succeed as
pilots or sportsmen or in work demanding special talents or
great accuracy. They may appear cool and difficult to understand, but they have the tolerance and gentleness to put up

with a great deal. They are able to display their abilities to the best if they find a person who understands their personalities. Though they tend to conceal their feelings in love, when they meet an ideal person, they become extremely passionate and self-sacrificing.

The leader and helpmate

The highly unusual *masukake* pattern is one in which the Life, Intellect, and Emotion Lines coalesce and is often seen in families in which there are scholars, geniuses, and people of great technical ability who lead highly individual lives (FIG. 127). Though superficially ordinary, they often are extremely persevering, capable of bold acts, and endowed with the amazing power to awe people that makes them good leaders. Such people frequently succeed in politics and big business. Because of their wonderful charm, they are very popular, though hesitancy to display emotion makes them seem cool in personal relations. They often succeed, but it sometimes takes them a long time to recover from a slump. Because they take a long time to select a partner, they usually marry late. It is highly likely that marriage will be a success if the partner is a person with the same *masukake* pattern or with a pattern in which the initial parts of Life and Intellect Lines are separated. Women with the *masukake* pattern are of the helpmate type who assist their husbands in getting ahead in the world. Often a match between an unrefined person and a person with such a pattern enables both to manifest their good points.

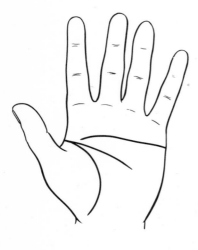

Fig. 127   The leader and helpmate

The type that is lucky to find collaborators

A Fate Line rising from the hypothenar indicates a person who succeeds better through popularity and the help of others than on his own (FIG. 128). A line of this kind is sometimes called the Popularity Line and is ideal for people who wish to become entertainers or engage in other lines of work in which popularity is important. It is vital that such people maintain smooth relations with others. Beside this line is a parallel Fate Line. If the two are close together, chances are good for success with the cooperation of others since, in these cases, unexpected material or financial assistance and potent words of advice are often forthcoming. Instead of trying to do things themselves, such people should discuss their actions with others. But, in the case of joint work, the partner should be selected carefully. The time for such action

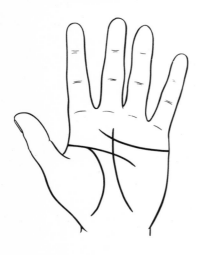

Fig. 128   The type that is lucky to find collaborators

should be judged on the age-division method of the Fate Line
(see FIG. 110).

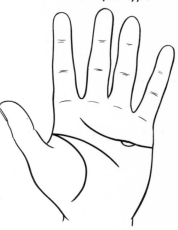

*Fig. 129   The easily
betrayed type*

The easily betrayed type

In palmistry, islandlike configurations are generally interpreted
as negative indications of harm or trouble. When they appear
on the Emotion Line, they may indicate hereditary heart
trouble but may also mean an unpleasant turn in personal
relations (FIG. 129). People in whom the end of the Emotion
Line is clean are said to have been blessed in their upbringing.
But islandlike marks on that line often suggest the likelihood
of trouble in love and marriage or of betrayal by others or
some other unhappiness. In such circumstances, judgment
should be made on the basis of the age-division of the Emotion Line (FIG. 130). A vertical crease that severs the Emotion
Line too means a breakdown in human relations or despair
in love.

*Fig. 130   Age-division
of the Emotion
Line*

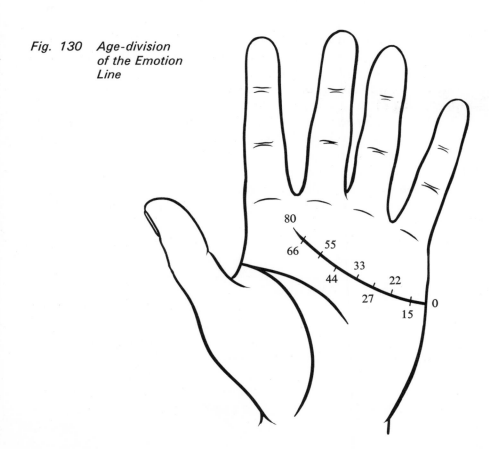

Judging Sexual and Romantic Inclinations on the Basis of the Palm

In the time of Napoleon, palmistry became widely popular because of the great interest people in aristocratic and high-ranking military circles demonstrated in love. Palmists were familiar sights in salons. They play a part in the novels of Oscar Wilde (1854–1900); and Le Norman, the palmist regularly employed by Napoleon's empress Josephine, was famous.

A similar tendency had prevailed, however, as early as 1692, when was published *Chiromancie Royale*, which is given over almost entirely to love and romantic relations between men and women. A small, illustrated book that could be carried easily on the person, it was quite practical. People with love troubles could refer to it or use it in reading the palm of the person to whom they felt attracted. Recently, a more versatile approach has come to be expected. For instance, Noël Jacquin has done research on the palm and homosexuality and other irregular sexual practices.

As has already been explained, the hand reflects much about the individual's emotional and physical condition. Similarly it reveals much about sexual awareness and desires. Creases in the hands, which are usually numerous and fine in women and few but clear in men, are related to hormone secretion. The little and ring fingers are especially strongly tied to sexual awareness and, in medical terms as well, are connected with the lower part of the body. Moving the little finger produces the Marriage Line. Wide motion of the little and ring fingers produces the Emotion Line. The thumb and the zone at its base are related to physical strength and stamina and are underdeveloped in thin people. W. S. Schlegel has medically demonstrated the relation between sex and the size of the hand. Marital frustration and divorce are common in husbands and wives in whom the peripheral measurements of the hands are radically different.

The material in the following pages has never been published in Japan before.

The Mount of Venus and Female Sex—*Understanding sexual development in the female*

The part of the hand marked (A) is called the Mount of Venus; the one marked (B) is called the Mount of the Moon (FIG. 131). In women, when the hand is gripped so that the two come together, the bulge formed in the center of the palm is profoundly related to the developmental condition of the female sexual organ. For instance, if the two mounts fail to come together when the hand is gripped firmly, the sexual organ is underdeveloped and loose. If the two come together, the sexual organ is well developed. The mount is large in large people and small in smaller ones. Both mounts lose fleshiness with advancing age.

Fig. 131 *The Mounts of Venus and the Moon*

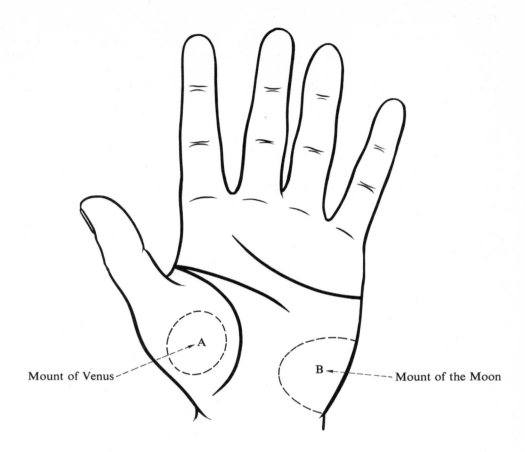

Mount of Venus- - - - - - - - - - - - A

B - - - - - - - - Mount of the Moon

The Mount of Venus and the thumb

The clenched fist, said to be comparable in size to the individual's heart, reveals the development of the uterus and vagina, degree of sexual passion, and the tightness of the vagina.

1) Women in whom the thumb comes inside the four fingers when the fist is clenched are tight and reach climax quickly but thoroughly dislike making passionate sounds and prefer to hold back and refrain from revealing themselves in what they consider lewd postures.

2) Women in whom the thumb comes on the outside of the four fingers and extends to the middle finger when the fist is clenched raise their voices and move vigorously during sex in the satisfaction of their own desires. They tend to be sexually slightly self-centered.

3) Women in whom the thumb reaches the index finger when the fist is clenched allow things to take their own course. They are perfectly clear in their likes and dislikes but sometimes cause men trouble by making hysterical displays.

Creases on the inner side of the Life Line that indicate sexual proclivities
A horizontal crease cutting across the Life Line
The most famous of the numerous creases formed on the inner side (Mount of Venus) of the Life Line is the *Via Lascivia*, a horizontal line cutting across the Life Line (FIG. 132-a). It is found in woman who enjoy a free, untrammeled sex life and deliberately seek thrills and adventure. If she were a real person, Lady Chatterley would no doubt have this line on her palm. Men in whom it occurs grow bored with ordinary married life.

Crease inside of and parallel with the Life Line
Called the Infidelity Line (FIG. 132-b), this crease occurs in people who, unable to control mounting frustration and desire, seek thrills in infidelity and philandering. Furthermore, such people usually possess abundant sexual stamina. Women in whom it occurs are often irresistible to men.

Chainlike marks in the creases at the base of the thumb.
Called Family Rings, these chainlike marks occur at the base of the thumb and

Fig. 132   Creases on the inner side of the Life Line that indicate sexual proclivities

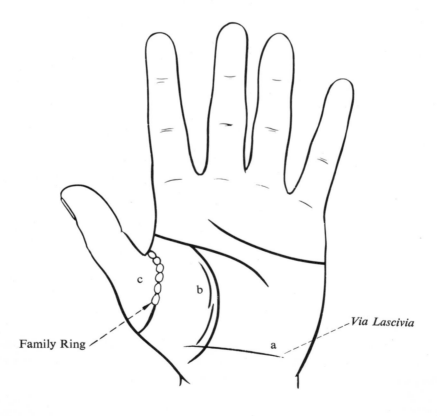

usually consist of one or two links (FIG. 132-c). Women in whom there are more than four clear links become pregnant easily and must take careful precautions if they do not want children.

Compatibility Revealed in the Intellect Line

The three forms of the Intellect Line (H, O, and L) reveal similarities and differences between men and women in sexual attitude and romantic expression.

In the combinations in this and the following section, the male comes first and the female second.

O – O
Though sometimes mannered, couples of this kind can fall in love intensely. They tend to become fat and to lose interest quickly but are able to love each other still, even without sex.

O – H
Women in these couples can become frustrated or attracted to other men. They are naturally endowed with the technical skills to give men pleasure and, once in love, find it difficult to part.

O – L
This is an ideal pairing. The woman tends to rely on and trust the man, who, for his part, has the masculine trait of wanting to protect the woman. Such people are strong when exposed to danger, and their love only heightens when rivals appear on the scene.

H – O
The man is very masculine, and the woman very feminine. Generally the man forcefully takes the lead, and initial sexual intercourse can take a form similar to the violation of a doe by a wild animal. Though the woman dislikes this at first, gradually she comes to give her best for the sake of the man.

H – H
This kind of couple becomes passionate fast and then cools off speedily. They have many liaisons and are sexually as dramatic as the people who appear in pornography.

H – L
The woman is strongly attracted at first but easily becomes dissatisfied and insecure. Couples of this kind agree better when they are of widely different ages. When they are of roughly the same age they tend to quarrel and be irritable.

L – O

The man is delicate, gentle, and considerate; the woman is domestic and likes to take care of her husband and family. A man with such a wife is extremely lucky.

L – H

Though secretly disliking it, the man leads the woman, who is usually either actually or psychologically older. Couples of this kind are often irritable because their sex life is unsatisfying.

L – L

Because they tire easily, couples of this kind avoid sexual excess. Their relation can easily become Platonic, and they find satisfaction from merely talking and kissing. They are lonely whenever apart.

Sex and the Emotion Line

Of the three basic lines in the palm, the Emotion Line is most valuable in judging styles of romantic and sexual expression and therefore in determining compatibility.

The simplicity or complexity of the Emotion Line reveals sexuality and intensity of interest in the opposite sex. People in whom the line is a gentle, simple curve are ordinary in this respect and have little interest in the unusual.

I – I

Couples of this kind have orthodox sexual interests but fortunately agree on the matter. They have mouths of a similar size and lips of a similar thickness and are sexually highly compatible. They are satisfied with intercourse once a week and fully enjoy it when they have it. They like sex in a brightly lighted room and manifest maximum interest in the sixty-nine position.

I – II

The woman shows faint interest in sex. Although highly excitable to stimulation in the back and hips, she is cold when actual intercourse begins. She will flatly refuse anything but the ordinary positions and has so many reservations that the male partner finds her unsatisfying and difficult to deal with. Compatibility takes a long time to achieve.

I – III

Couples of this kind long to be compatible. Often they feel they were fated to be in love from first sight. Such couples can be certain of satisfying the woman's sexual desires completely. In love-making, the woman likes to be embraced from the back.

II – I

Couples of this kind can tolerate limitations on frequency of intercourse. Since they enjoy talking about work and outside interests more than about sex, their love can be deepened by sharing occupations, hobbies, or fields of study. If the woman is unfaithful or shows romantic interest in someone else, the man can become interested in homosexual love.

II – II

Both have little interest in sex and do not indulge to excess. They can love without physical excitement and get along well as long as they have no serious money or other worries. It takes a long time for people of this kind to discover the true joy of sex.

II – III

Constantly irritable and unsettled, such couples frequently complain, have clashes of opinion, and quarrel without apparent reason. While interested in her hobbies and in fashion, the woman often fails to understand the man. Both parties tend to be shut up in their own shells.

III – I

Totally lacking in understanding of men, the woman is repelled by physical contact. Though she may try hard to become technically skillful, both partners usually find little satisfaction.

III – II

Hurrying only makes things worse for people of this kind. Though they seem to have fallen in love at first sight, they are easily betrayed and readily lose hope. Often they discover their differences the first time they become naked together. Quarrels increase thereafter.

III – III

Both-partners can become virtually enslaved to sex and can enjoy staying in bed all day long. They delight in trying different things and are perfectly suited to what is called the age of sex. If they ever know frustration, it is sexual.

Fig. 133 *Creases indica-
ting abundant
opportunities*

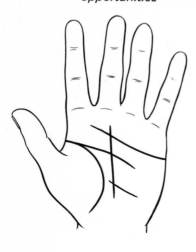

Fig. 134

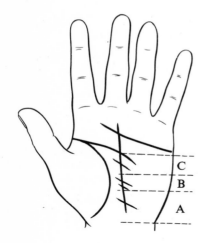

Palmistry and Fortune in Marriage

Abundant opportunities

A well-fleshed palm (hypothenar) and a long, clear crease extending upward toward the Fate Line (FIG. 133) indicate abundant opportunities for love and marriage. People who have this line in both hands frequently marry after falling passionately in love. When the hypothenar line is single and clear, the person will be ardently loved and desired by another. Both arranged and romantic marriages are likely to succeed for such people.

The position of the hypothenar, however, alters the meaning of this crease. FIG. 134 is useful in analyzing this position. The hand is divided into three zones. A line divides the distance between the wrist line and the point of intersection between Intellect and Fate Lines in half. The entire bottom half is zone (A). The upper half is subdivided into a lower band called (B) and an upper band called (C).

When creases are numerous in the (A) zone (or when there is one single line and it occurs in the [A] zone), the person is likely to marry early, probably before the age of twenty often with a partner with whom contact was first made in the teens. When there is no line on the hypothenar except in this zone, if the person fails to marry quite young, it will take years to find a partner; and perhaps the chance for marriage will be lost altogether. Before twenty or, at the latest, by twenty-two is the ideal time for such people to wed.

For both men and women, several lines in the (B) zone (or one line in the [B] zone and none elsewhere) indicate marriage at what is considered the normal time of life; that is, between twenty and twenty-five or six. The clearer the hypothenar lines the better the chances for happiness in love. But a large number of lines in this region suggests relations with so many members of the opposite sex that chances for marriage are lost. In many instances, beautiful, intelligent women who ought to be popular with men but nonetheless remain single have this kind of palm pattern.

Numerous creases extending from the hypothenar into the (C) zone with no creases or very few in the (A) and (B) zones indicate that chances of meeting the ideal partner and being happily married are greater at older ages. Such people should concentrate their energy on work until about twenty-seven. Too early an eagerness to marry invites misunderstanding from members of the opposite sex. And an early wedding could lead to unexpected trouble.

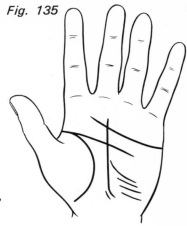

Fig. 135

People with the palm pattern in Fig. 135, in which there are more than two lines rising from the hypothenar, are extremely popular with the opposite sex and enjoy being so to the extent that they are fickle and unfaithful to their many boyfriends or girlfriends. Among the lines on the hypothenar, the longest and clearest is related to the relation that will lead to marriage.

When, as in Fig. 136, the line from the hypothenar crosses the Fate Line, the individual is strongly loved by members of the opposite sex. And, when this pattern occurs in both hands, the likelihood of marriage is great. Even when this line is long, however, if it fails to cross the Fate Line, in spite of ardent love from the opposite sex, various obstacles greatly lower the chances of marriage.

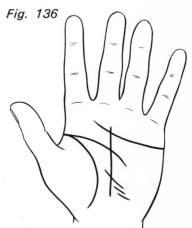

Fig. 136

The type that has little chance of marriage

Although the usual trend is for many fine creases to appear in the center of the palm, in some people, these creases are either few or totally absent. People in whom horizontal or slanting lines in the hypothenar are either few or missing (Fig. 137) are misunderstood by the opposite sex; and their affections are frequently one-sided. When this pattern occurs in both hands, the individual's personality or life environment is the reason why the opposite sex is not attracted and opportunities for marriage are not forthcoming. In some instances, altering the rhythm of the life environment by such simple steps as rearranging the furniture and changing one's way of dressing or hairstyle can improve chances for marriage. Furthermore, such persons must have the patience to wait until these lines appear in the hypothenar. In hands of this kind, if there are no horizontal creases at the base of the middle finger, often the person will concentrate more on interest in work than on marriage. Under these circumstances it is wiser to take one's time and conclude an arranged marriage than to rush impetuously into a romantic one.

Fig. 137 *The type that has little chance of marriage*

Creases on the hypothenar of the right hand but none on the hypothenar of the left hand mean that the person fails to be aware of the love another has for him or her or that the lover is so close that the emotions are being overlooked. An absence of creases on the hypothenar of both hands and the presence of a cross-shaped crease at the base of the index finger mean that a chance for marriage is imminent or that

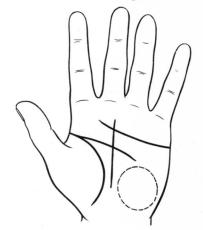

an acquaintance is about to bring news that could lead to wedlock.

The type prone to love troubles

The highly unusual pattern in which islandlike configurations (FIG. 138) appear on the side of the hypothenar indicates plenty of chance for marriage and passionate, but troubled, romance with the opposite sex. For instance, a person with this pattern may fall passionately in love with another person who is married and has children. Or economic burdens could pose problems. People in whom these islandlike configurations occur at a point corresponding to their own age fall passionately in love to the extent that they overlook the objections of all relatives and associates. But such a love affair will take a long time to be resolved and is unlikely to be fruitful. In these hand patterns, if the Fate Line is clear in both palms, it is strongly possible that other chances will present themselves even after one unhappy love affair.

Generally women with many creases extending from the hypothenar are bewitching and popular with men. If they occur in this region, islandlike configurations are likely to occur elsewhere as well, sometimes in the so-called Girdle of Venus, a semicircular line at the base of the middle finger usually consisting of one or two lines (FIG. 138). People with this pattern frequently suffer bitterly in love or seek an adventurous sex life. Women of this type fall in love with younger men and are determined to marry them over the objections of their parents.

Caution is essential to overcome possible trouble if one of a pair of lovers manifests this pattern. If it occurs in the man's hand, the trouble will arise from the woman and vice-versa.

The type prone to marital difficulties

The crease extends from the hypothenar, crosses the Fate Line, but beyond the intersection the Fate Line is blank (FIG. 139). This pattern indicates smooth sailing during courtship and proposal but trouble, material or psychological, a few years after marriage. If the pattern appears in both man and wife, it is essential to reconsider life-style plans, discuss matters with friends and relatives, and exercise cool judgment. Unfortunately, however, usually people who manifest this pattern are unwilling to accept even the best advice. Since it is possible, with joint work, to overcome the difficulty, when financial trouble occurs after about three years of marriage, it is of the

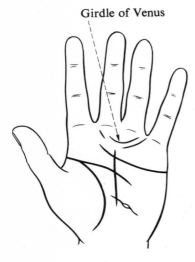

Fig. 138   The type prone to love troubles

Girdle of Venus

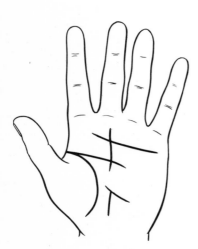

Fig. 139   The type prone to marital difficulties

greatest importance to give up frivolous pleasures and be patient and persevering. Characteristically, people with this pattern tend to look at married life through rose-colored glasses and then to be disappointed by the discrepancy between their dreams and actuality.

The type prone to unmarried cohabitation

The line from the hypothenar extends in the direction of the Fate Line but breaks off midway (FIG. 140). This pattern occurs often in young couples who, working in the same office, fall in love but encounter all kinds of obstacles. They associate with each other passionately and for a long time but are unable to make up their minds to marry. This often causes the man to worry and to suffer an on-the-job slump. Under such circumstances, it is a good idea to seek the help of seniors and friends. Both partners will be hurt if things drag on as they are. It is possible that the woman will be willing to live with the man as if they were married though formally out of wedlock. This palm pattern is characteristic of people for whom initial sexual relations develop into love.

The happily married type

Star-shaped configurations appear at the point where a very clear line extending from the side of the hypothenar intersects with the Fate Line (FIG. 141). When this pattern appears in people whose youth has been filled with hardship and suffering, they can look forward to meeting a member of the opposite sex who surpasses all their dreams and with whom they will find happiness through marriage.

The modern Cinderella type

In this pattern the horizontal line extending from the base of the little finger—the Marriage Line—is extremely long (FIG. 142-A). Usually, the longer this line, the better the chances of making a successful marriage after a very passionate romance. Women with this line marry more often romantically than by arrangement. People with patterns resembling the one shown in FIG. 142-A are very prone to intense romance. This pattern reveals a very long Marriage Line extending all the way to the base of the ring finger and a diagonal crease intersecting the Fate Line in the center of the palm. Such people are only made more passionate by objections voiced by friends and relatives.

Sometimes the end of the Marriage Line intersects with the

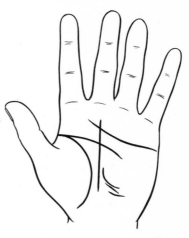

Fig. 140　The type prone to unmarried cohabitation

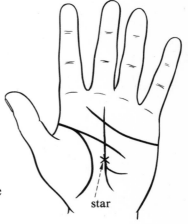

Fig. 141　The happily married type

star

*Fig. 142   The modern
Cinderella type*

A

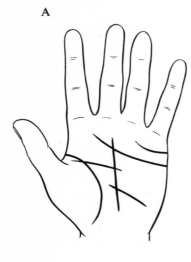

B

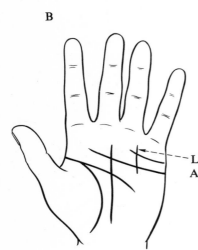

‑ ‑ Line of
Apollo

vertical line (Line of Apollo) at the base of the ring finger (FIG. 142-B). People with this pattern, though inconspicuous at the start, often find great wealth or fame as a consequence of marriage. Women in whose hands the Marriage and Line of Apollo intersect in a cross and the Intellect Line begins well below the Life Line often marry millionaires or are desired by monarchs. For a long time, this pattern has been interpreted in this way and has been referred to as the pattern of women who marry into the purple.

The type prone to marital instability
This pattern, in which the Marriage Line, which runs horizontally at the base of the little finger, is bent, occurs with comparatively high frequency. Its characteristics depend on the way in which it curves. In the pattern in Fig. 143-A, the Marriage Line turns downward toward the Life Line and intersects with the Emotion Line. The old-fashioned interpretation of the line as indicating divorce is discredited by the comparative frequency with which this pattern occurs in men and women over forty who are leading happily married lives. But it does occur often in people who lack sexual stamina or are very fastidious in connection with sex. In such conditions, attitudes toward sex mean that married life may run smoothly or be in for trouble. For instance, when a woman with this palm pattern marries a man with islandlike configurations on the Marriage Line, differing attitudes toward

Fig. 143   The type prone to marital instability

A   B

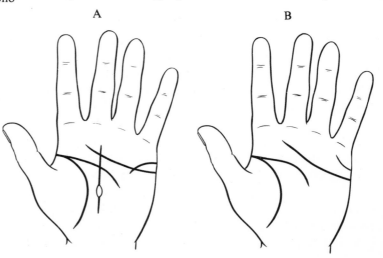

sex can mean mutual frustration and an unhappy married life. But, when the downward curving Marriage Line occurs in both members of a couple, married life is often smooth and satisfying. In such cases, people who seek psychological more than physical satisfaction have an excellent chance of being happy.

Similarly, when the hand of one marital partner demonstrates a pattern in which the Marriage Line curves downward and there are islands on the Fate Line, trouble between the sexes can lead to divorce. When one of a couple manifests this pattern, the greatest caution is called for in all matters concerning the opposite sex.

The pattern in FIG. 143-B, in which the Marriage Line curves upward toward the base of the little finger, frequently indicates a personality directly opposite to the one represented by the pattern in FIG. 143-A. Such people are deeply interested in sex. Women with this upward curving Marriage Line cannot be satisfied with one man alone and become captivated by sexual techniques. They have both abundant physical stamina and desires that, exceeding the bounds of rational control, verge on the licentious. Once they know the joy of sex, they cannot suppress their desire. This too is a pattern that Lady Chatterley would no doubt manifest if she were a real person.

Instead of settling down with one woman in marriage, men with this pattern often remain bachelors, enjoying sex with a large number of women and sometimes develop interest in homosexual love.

Fig. 144 The type that requires cooling off

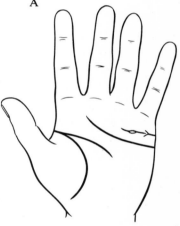

A

The type that requires cooling off

People in whom the end of the Marriage Line splits into two branches experience periodic (after three or nine years, for instance) slumps during which they become frustrated and seriously contemplate divorce. Sometimes, however, during these low periods, they avoid this drastic step by concentrating their attention on work or children.

If they persist in the idea of divorce during a slump, people in whom islandlike configurations occur beyond the split end of the Marriage Line (FIG. 144-A) must be prepared to lose temporarily all the fame and position they have previously attained. People in whom a long, clear line appears beyond the split end of the Marriage Line (FIG. 144-B), however, may look forward to restoring happy marital relations if, at slump time, they separate temporarily from their spouses and allow

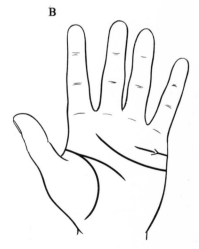

B

C

Fig. 145   The sexually
             frustrated type

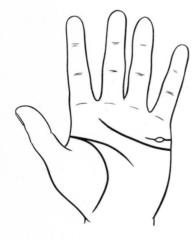

themselves a period in which to cool off. They may avoid divorce if they plan a suitable strategy.

A crease curving downward from the split end of the Marriage Line and crossing the Emotion Line (FIG. 144-C) indicates serious frustration and sexual incompatibility demanding control of desire and understanding of the partner's sexual needs. Nonetheless, people with this pattern need not hesitate to marry. These lines can be eliminated by altering one's approach to marriage or by attaining a state of mental stability.

When these lines, accompanied by islandlike configurations, appear in both hands, marriage plans should be carried out slowly and cautiously. In such instances, the longer the courtship, the more stable the marriage.

The sexually frustrated type

Islandlike configurations usually mean trouble. In this case they suggest obstacles to love and marriage. This pattern occurs in three variations (FIG. 145): (a) the islandlike configurations occur at the end of the Marriage Line; (b) they occur somewhere in the course of; and (c) they appear at the beginning of the Marriage Line.

In the case of the (a) type, married life goes smoothly at first, and the partners enjoy satisfying sex. After three or five years, however, monotony sets in. And, earlier than is usually the case, married life enters a phase of doldrums generally because of sexual frustration on the part of one partner. In this period of lassitude, the couple begins to seek fresh stimulation. The problem can be overcome for some people by redecorating the bedroom. For a long time, this combination of Marriage Line and islandlike configurations has been interpreted to mean divorce.

In the case of the (b) variation, in about the seventh year, premarriage troubles and distrust revive to cause a formerly happily married couple to begin suddenly snarling at each other and often to show interest in extramarital relations.

Though not at the beginning, for people who have the (c) variation of the pattern, as time passes, incompatibility becomes a problem. Owing to differences of opinion and interests, quarrels and squabbles are frequent. In these instances, mutual understanding is essential.

The appearance of islandlike creases on the Marriage Line means sex-related problems. Often an apparently virtuous and modest person who manifests this pattern will suddenly dis-

cover someone appealing and become so passionately infatuated that matters proceed to sex.

As this discussion should make clear, the Marriage Line
relates many things, including of course love and marriage,
but extending to the individual's interest in the opposite sex
and concealed expectations.

A small number of Marriage Lines (one or two) and a long,
clear Marriage Line generally mean an emotional, passionately
sexual character and the likelihood that the person will take
the marital chance offered and make a happy married life.
A larger number of these lines reveals a high degree of interest
in sex and fickleness, a tendency to infatuation, and an inability to settle down. Such people suffer before marriage and
find it difficult to select partners in marital arrangements.
Sometimes the opportunity to wed escapes them completely.

Usually, a long, clear Marriage Line reveals a strongly
emotional character; and a short, fine one relative indifference.
People who lack Marriage Lines completely are uninterested
in the opposite sex, prefer work to sexual relations, and seek
psychological instead of physical pleasure. Incidentally, Marriage Lines appear in the palms of chimpanzees and gorillas.

It is a mistake to attempt to judge the number of marriages
a person will have from the Marriage Line, which is best used
to determine the individual's attitude toward the opposite sex
and outlooks on marriage and the family.

The Type Prone to Unfaithfulness

This pattern has creases like (a) or (b) on the inner side of the
Life Line (FIG. 146-A). The vertical crease on the well-fleshed
area inside the Life Line, called the Mount of Venus, is important in determining the individual's interest in the opposite
sex and in being unfaithful to spouse or steady partner. It
reveals whether one's present sweetheart is interested in
another person or is being unfaithful. When the Mount of
Venus is well developed, a line appearing inside the Life Line
indicates powers of physical resistance and the fighting power
to obtain desired objects and goals. Ancient palmistry interpreted this line as indicating whether a woman would find
emotional happiness.

Many men and women in whom there is a crease parallel
to the Life Line on the Mount of Venus (as in [a]) and in
whom the Marriage Line curves as in (c) and extends toward
the base of the ring finger are highly passionate and strongly

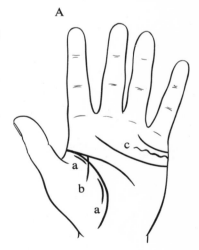

*Fig. 146 The type prone to
unfaithfulness*

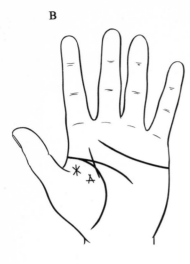

B

attracted to the opposite sex. They fall in love at first sight; after fairly brief association, their love blossoms into a grand passion. Often, even after marriage, they continue to be interested in other people and are prone to extramarital affairs. When the line on the Mount of Venus crosses the Life Line (b), extramarital affairs can become serious enough to cause trouble between man and wife. These lines (a) and (b) on the Mount of Venus are the most reliable hint of infidelity in both men and women.

Sometimes, the line on the Mount of Venus assumes a star or triangular form (FIG. 146-B), which indicates a totally unexpected meeting with an ideal partner or a sudden proposal. In such instances, association with someone met on a trip or on the job can develop into marriage. The Mount of Venus reveals justness and passion. A person who has many complex creases on it leads a highly individualistic life.

Advance Signs of Ill Fortune

Palmistry and fortune-telling have survived for many centuries, often in spite of oppression and condemnation as a tool of the devil, because all human beings want to obtain fundamentally unobtainable information about the unknown tomorrow. More specifically, people are interested mostly in knowing when current good fortune will turn to ill fortune. It was in the hope of learning this that the European royalty and aristocracy of the eighteenth century put great credence in the pronouncements of astrologers and palmists. The man who is king today avidly seeks to find out if he will soon be ruled by another. At an earlier time, it had been the aristocracy who supported Nostradamus and made it possible for him to become famous. Though they might otherwise have gone unnoticed, Nostradamus's predictions in his book, *The Centuries*, caused a stir because they attacked the pope and foresaw the end of Christianity and the downfall of the French monarchy.

Fig. 147

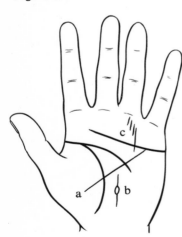

The pattern of the palm too can provide accurate information about imminent ill fortune. Long experience examining and surveying the palms of people who have suddenly fallen on rationally unexplainable hard luck has shown that characteristic presages, not occurring in other people, can be seen in the lines of their palms.

Signs in the Palm

A) Of the many indications of bad fortune appearing in the palm, the primary key is the long line extending from the base of the thumb toward the Life Line (FIG. 147-a). If this line, which is called the Obstacle Line, is long and deep, trouble may be in store. If it extends far enough to stop the Fate Line, trouble may occur in daily life, work may be adversely influenced, or outside elements may spell the ruination of business. In such cases, great caution is warranted in connection with scandal and women. Changes in life-style can shorten or completely eliminate this line.

B) If islandlike configurations occur along the important Fate Line, the individual may experience grave damage in work or social life (FIG. 147-b). The person may be held responsible for things that are not actually his responsibility and may encounter repeated unpleasantness over an extended period. Meditation is helpful in softening this hard luck.

C) The appearance of many fine lines in the vicinity of the Line of Apollo means an increasing tendency to spend money extravagantly (FIG. 147-c). Because of the danger of spending on others or of exhausting the entire present store, it is wise for such people not to carry large amounts of cash when they go out. Altering attitudes toward money is a key to improving fortune.

People in whom the Fate Line is broken in several places cannot hold a job for long and experience periodic work slumps, during which they lose all initiative. They tend to be easily attracted to other companies and to the idea of changing jobs and often do things only halfway. They will find that caution, sincere devotion to their own work, and the acquisition of technical skills or other qualifications will affect their fortunes favorably.

D) The appearance of X-shaped marks in the vicinity of the Hope Line, which ascends from the Life Line, suggests failure owing either to excess ambition or the creation of enemies (FIG. 148-d). Overconfidence can lead to regrets. If these X marks appear at a time when fortune is waxing, a sudden turn for the worse may be in store.

E) Frequently people in whom a large number of fine creases ascend from the Life Line overextend themselves to the point of failure (FIG. 148-e). Such persons are the type who take on too much work from too many people and then suffer failure. Their expenditures too increase. But the appear-

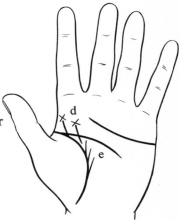

Fig. 148

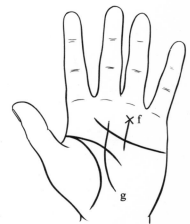

Fig. 149

Fig. 150

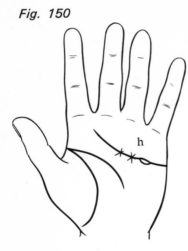

Fig. 151

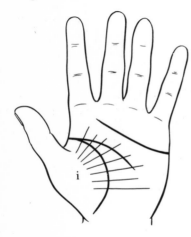

Fig. 152

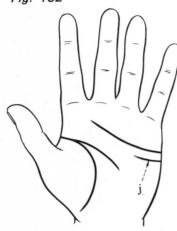

ance of a long line in this crease indicates an improvement in fortune and appointment to a position of responsibility.

F) The appearance of an X at the end of the Line of Apollo (FIG. 149-f) can mean financial good luck and the unexpected turning up of a large amount of money, which ultimately, however, becomes the cause of failure and downfall. People manifesting this pattern sometimes ruin themselves by borrowing money and should be extremely cautious of gambling.

G) Generally, people in whom the Fate Line curves (FIG. 149-g) do all they can to help and encourage others but sometimes go too far and are consequently abandoned by the very people they assist. They must not allow themselves to be cajoled since, though things may go well at the outset, human relations will deteriorate later and can continue to do so.

H) People in whom an X or island configuration occurs along the Emotion Line are often in for betrayal or other unpleasantness in human relations (FIG. 150-h). The betrayal may be by a person on the job who in the past has been thought a trusted associate. Since they are very trusting, such people are often used by others for selfish advantage.

I) People with creases radiating into the center of the palm from the base of the thumb often fail to utilize their own abilities completely because of a complex about their education or social background (FIG. 151-i). Or they expose themselves by being pretentious. They will be better trusted on the job if, instead of boasting, they have confidence in themselves as they truly are and do all they can to improve.

J) People with a horizontal line immediately below the Emotion Line invite animosity from seniors and older people by always resisting what is told them (FIG. 152-j). This proclivity sometimes leads to demotions on the job. They must be very careful in their manner of speaking and expressing their feelings. When drinking, they can break out in a sudden rage and lose control of their emotions.

Types of Signs of Ill Luck

Sometimes called the Occupation Line since it manifests changes in work, the Fate Line alters to reveal alterations in life-style and advancing age. The appearance of an island configuration in the zone of the Fate Line corresponding to

current age often indicates poor physical condition or unexpected trouble in human relations (FIG. 153). Generally
regarded as harbingers of ill fortune, these islandlike configurations can mean that nothing undertaken will succeed or that
things that first go well will take a turn for the worse. It is
wise to check both hands for them since they sometimes occur
on the right hand and not on the left. When they occur on
the Fate Line, they mean that the person has trouble with
human relations owing to an inability to express himself accurately to others. When they are on both hands, no undertaking goes as planned; and the person must wait either until
the islands vanish or are no longer at the position corresponding to current age. Patience is essential since it may be necessary to wait three years. But it should be remembered that
virtually no misfortunes or unpleasantnesses in life last longer
than that.

People more than forty years of age with these islandlike
configurations can no longer expect things to go as well as they
have been going. Their plans will meet with unexpected reversals, and they themselves will argue and have differences
of opinion with associates. It is essential for them to make
maximum efforts to assure that people around them understand their thoughts and goals. Before undertaking anything
new, they should think it out carefully and ask the opinions
of others. The initiation of any big plan may have negative
effects and result in a loss of labor. Any plan to alter residence or occupation should be postponed for a year.

Sometimes a short, slanting line will be seen either under
or above the islandlike configuration (FIG. 154). A palm
pattern like the one in (A) often means unexpected good luck
with the opposite sex and love and marriage that inspire
enthusiasm for work. Sometimes, however, it means that
things that go well at first deteriorate and have an adverse
effect on work. To rectify the situation, problems in relations
with the opposite sex must first be resolved. It is necessary to
postpone pleasure with the opposite sex when it means a turn
for the worse in previously good work and financial conditions.

Short lines appearing above the islandlike configuration, as
in (B), indicate a sudden turn for the better in the fortune of
a person who has experienced unexpected trouble on the job,
repeated personal problems, or continued financial losses.
The power of a sweetheart or other member of the opposite
sex often brings about the change. In spite of a degree of in-

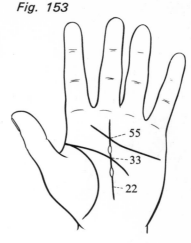

Fig. 153

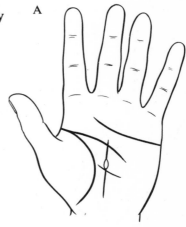

Fig. 154

A

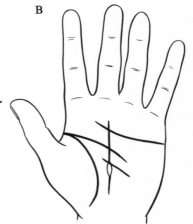

B

Fig. 155

A

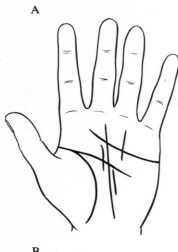

B

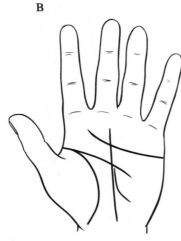

C

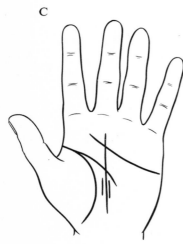

security, it is important to have the courage to go ahead boldly with plans to marry. For married people, the help of a spouse or mutual encouragement can provide the strength needed to overcome difficulties.

The Type That Succeeds with the Help of Others

The appearance of a short crease parallel to the Fate Line means that assistance from others is forthcoming or that the help of others will make success possible for a person who heretofore has failed in everything. Such people should turn to seniors or others for counsel and advice instead of trying to do everything on their own.

These lines paralleling the Fate Line may take several forms and may occur on the thumb side or on the ring-finger side (FIG. 155-A). Appearing on the ring-finger side, the lines often mean that a powerful helper will make possible success on the job. If this line is accompanied by a clear Line of Apollo (vertical line below the ring finger), material and financial as well as psychological assistance is likely. When the line parallel to the Fate Line appears on the thumb side, however, the individual will help others or provide financial assistance enabling friends or relatives to find a chance for success. Though this outlay may seem a waste at first, ultimately it will bring its own reward. People of this type frequently look out for the welfare of others who are not their family responsibility.

French palmistry interprets the pattern in which a line parallel to the Fate Line extends from the hypothenar as indicating assistance from the opposite sex or an unexpected opportunity in connection with love or marriage (FIG. 155-B). If it intersects with the Fate Line, this crease means that love and consideration from a member of the opposite sex will provide assistance leading to good fortune. Running parallel to the Fate Line, it indicates that a member of the opposite sex will have a positive effect on the individual's work. American palmistry researchers interpret this line to indicate trust and financial assistance from associates of the opposite sex. This line is considered to be especially auspicious and to reveal an improvement in fortune and is often seen in women who, like Cinderella, are loved by men of great wealth.

The very rare pattern in which lines parallel to the Fate Line extend from both the thumb and the hypothenar (FIG. 155-C) occurs in only one out of a hundred people and suggests excellent fortune in the form of an inheritance or sudden wealth from gambling or investments. A certain book on palmistry illustrates this with the story of a ten-year-old American orphan who suddenly inherited great wealth.

The Changing Fate Line

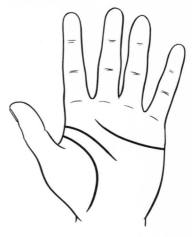

Fig. 156

As this discussion indicates, the Fate Line assumes so many forms and so clearly reflects the individual's life that palmistry might be said to consist fundamentally in investigating its characteristics. Furthermore, it changes with alterations in condition and fortune and is likely to be very different two or three months after an initial reading of a person's palm. When a person is experiencing poor luck or either is not putting his abilities to best use or is not in circumstances to do so, the Fate Line will be unclear or sometimes absent altogether.

The Fate Lines of the left and right hands may differ. For instance, it may be clear and indicative of good fortune in one and unclear or missing in the other. When this happens, the hand in which the line is vague or missing indicates current or near-future conditions.

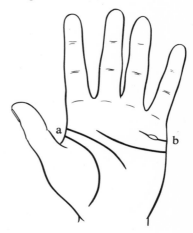

Fig. 157

Ill Fortune in Love and Marriage

People in whom the beginnings of the Life and Intellect Lines are separate, as in FIG. 156 are, highly emotional and often experience bad luck in love and marriage. If both members of a couple have this hand pattern, though it may start off with intense passion, their affair may end in quarrels, continuous troubles, and ultimate separation. Such people can, however, alter their fate by controlling their emotions.

When the Marriage Line assumes the islandlike configuration seen in FIG. 157, the individual has a difficult time getting married. Even should he love someone, such unforeseen obstacles as family objections or other romantic interests on the part of the partner prevent marriage. In such circumstances, people often form relations other than the usual marital ones or fall in love with two people at the same time.

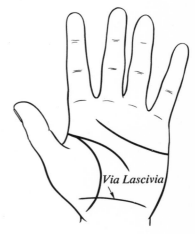

Fig. 158

People in whom the *Via Lascivia*—the horizontal line at the base of the thumb (FIG. 158), occurs dislike being forced into patterns, enjoy free love, and prefer cohabitation to marriage.

People in whom the Marriage Line is in the form of a chain or is twisted are sexually irresponsible and pleasure-loving. Lacking control over their desires, they often suffer as a consequence of immoral love affairs. Gaining control over sexual desires is the shortcut to changing fortune for such people.

Fig. 159

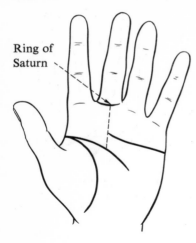

Ring of
Saturn

When the Emotion Line is so short that it extends only to a point below the middle finger (FIG. 159), the individual is poorly understood or even shunned by the opposite sex. Such people are emotionally changeable and clumsy at establishing personal relations. Though they think they are doing their best for the partner, things often do not go as they like; and they resort to excessive masturbation.

People in whom the Marriage Line (at the base of the little finger) is completely missing marry either late or not at all. When they fall in love, it is often unrequited. Others do not easily understand their feelings.

The presence of the Ring of Saturn, the semicircular crease at the base of the middle finger, indicates interest in homosexuality or such intense pleasure in unusual sexual practices that ordinary intercourse is unsatisfying.

An X at the ends of the slanting, intertwined lines on the right and left of the Fate Line (FIG. 160) indicates that grand passion will end tragically in unforeseen trouble.

In the pattern in FIG. 161, the Influence Line crosses the Fate Line but has an island on it. A man with this pattern who falls passionately in love may find that his sweetheart is betraying him, or some other kind of trouble may arise in connection with her.

A descending Marriage Line indicates faint interest in love and often a late marriage. Even when they marry early, people with this pattern easily become either frustrated or divorced. Probably only slightly interested in sex, they should not rush matters and will be happier if they marry late.

A Marriage Line split in two (FIG. 162) can indicate in-

Fig. 160

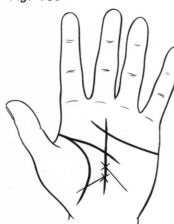

Fig. 161

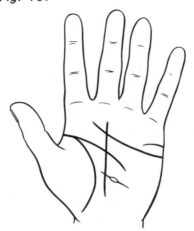

Fig. 162

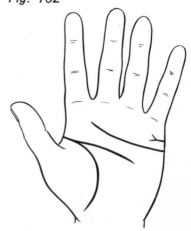

compatibility, separation, and possibly divorce. People with this pattern find that their most assiduous efforts to improve the situation only increase the partner's estrangement.

Alterations in the styles of married life have resulted in the appearance of palm patterns that did not exist in the past. For instance, this pattern is not introduced in old works on palmistry.

Signs of Physical Misfortune

A large island on the Health Line (FIG. 163), which extends from the base of the little finger toward the Life Line, means a general bodily upset largely influenced by psychological stress. In such instances, it is often more important to think of mental control than of the sickness itself.

Fine lines at the end of the Life Line (FIG. 164) indicate poor stomach condition and a constitution that tires easily and is nervous. In addition, they suggest a disruption of daily-life rhythm and illness during a journey.

An X along the Life Line or at the end of the Intellect Line (FIG. 165) indicates the need for caution to avoid injury, especially to the part of the body above the shoulders. In addition, it is related to illnesses requiring surgery.

Alteration of creases along the Life Line or appearance in its vicinity of new creases presages a change in condition or constitution. When these changes are for the worse, the color of the skin will darken. (It is important to remember that skin color and luster are related to general health.)

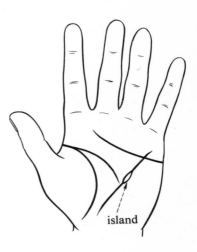

Fig. 163

island

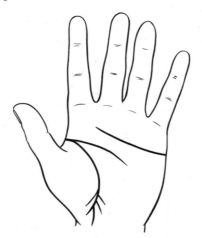

Fig. 164

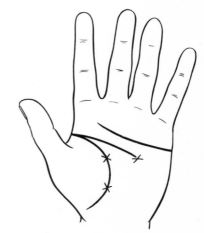

Fig. 165

Fig. 166

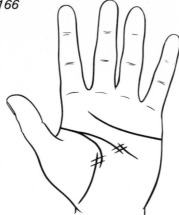

Fig. 167

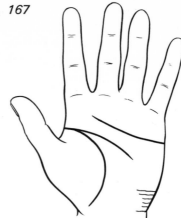

Fig. 168

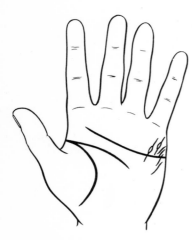

Fig. 169

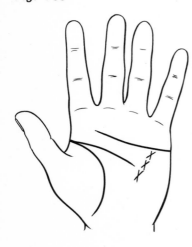

A fairly common phenomenon is the appearance of what is called a square on the Life Line or the Intellect Line (FIG. 166). This square often means a very close scrape with death or very serious surgery.

Many horizontal lines on the palm near the wrist (FIG. 167) are connected with the condition of the liver and indicate the need to be moderate in drinking and smoking. In addition, these lines reveal a tendency to seek stimulation and to over-indulge in alcohol, tobacco, and sometimes marijuana. When bodily condition is restored, these lines usually disappear.

An islandlike configuration or a bending crease (FIG. 168) at the base of the little finger indicates danger of venereal disease or often menstrual irregularity in women. In such cases the skin will be dark and rough.

An X between the Emotion and Intellect Lines (FIG. 169) suggests the danger of illness affecting the eyes or ears, usually influenced by fatigue.

Two vertically oriented lines at the bases of the little and ring fingers (FIG. 170) indicate weakness in the legs (in the left leg if the creases occur in the right hand and vice versa) and possible injury to the lower back and hips. The weakness is greater in proportion to the depth of the crease.

Fine lines like those in FIG. 171 appearing at the start of the Emotion Line indicate the need for caution in relation to cardiovascular illnesses. People with this pattern sometimes die suddenly of such sicknesses.

People with a large break or bend in the Intellect Line (FIG. 172) are prone to injury and often are the type that break bones on the ski slope.

The occurrence of several chainlike lines at the start of the

Fig. 170

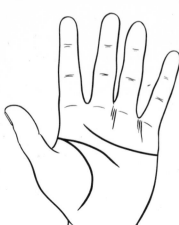

Fig. 171

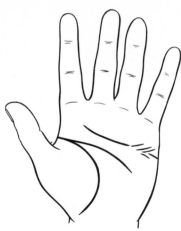

Fig. 172

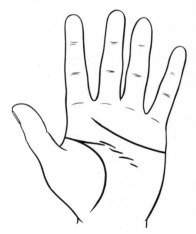

Life Line (FIG. 173) indicates weakness of the bronchial tubes, allergies, and asthma. Improvement in bodily condition alters these lines.

Persons whose Intellect Line curves deeply downward toward the Life Line (FIG. 174) are more cautious and suffer greater stress than ordinary individuals. They are irritable and insecure, and their illnesses are generally psychologically caused.

Many downward slanting lines on the Emotion Line (FIG. 175) indicate a constitution tending to weakness in the alimentary system and to sicknesses resulting from on-the-job stress and irritating personal relations. In these people too illness is often rooted in the emotions.

Fig. 173

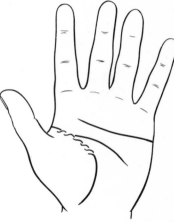

Fig. 174

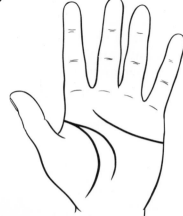

Fig. 175

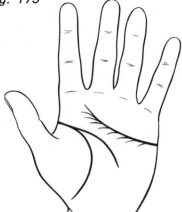

How the Diet Can Change Palm Patterns

I have already explained how altering personality, life-style, and environment can change palm patterns. Similarly, the diet can have an effect on them. For some years, Katsuzō Nishi, famous for the Nishi-style health system, and George Ohsawa, familiar to many people all over the world for his system of macrobiotics based on the oriental Yin-Yang philosophy, have insisted that this is true. In many countries, Ohsawa operates macrobiotic restaurants called Ohsawa Houses; and, in 1968, one was opened in the Mejiro district of Tokyo, where it enjoys great popularity among Japanese and non-Japanese alike.

Both the Nishi and the Ohsawa systems reject traditional Western meat-centered diets in favor of natural macrobiotic foods on the basis of the belief that eating habits going against the rules of nature are the cause of many of the illnesses plaguing our rapidly altering society—particularly of such things as cancer and diabetes.

Because of the elaborate way in which blood vessels and nerves are connected in them, the hands vividly reflect the state of the body's nourishment. And, because these nervous and vascular connections are different on the thumb and on the little-finger side of the hand, these sides exert influences on different parts of the body. This line of thought is assumed to be common sense in traditional Chinese medicine. For instance, acupuncture or moxa combustion are practiced on the base of the thumb to treat edema of the face because of the relations between these two parts of the body.

As has already been explained, the connections relating parts of the body are called meridians. From a region near the thumb arises the Greater Yin Lung Meridian, which extends to the lungs and large intestine. From the little-finger side of the hand arises the Lesser Yin Heart Meridian, which extends to the heart and small intestine. From the middle finger arises the Absolute Yin Pericardium Meridian, which is connected with the center of the body and the head.

Against the background of this medical philosophy has been evolved a system of determining the ways in which dietary habits affect the pattern of lines and creases in the palm. Because of its connections with the lungs and large intestine, the thumb is high in acid. Because of its relation to the small intestine, the little finger is high in alkali. Therefore when the body's acid content is high, the Life Line will be. deep and clear; and, when its alkali content is high, the Emotion Line, at the base of the little finger, will be clear.

Improving the Palm Pattern by Training the Mind

Psychological Method for Improving the Overall Palm Pattern

It is possible to change the palm pattern and alter future fate for the better in young children by submitting them to a course of psychological training. Vitalizing the various functions of the fingers and hands will improve the three basic lines of the palm pattern. To improve the overall pattern, however, requires manual movements representing total psychosomatic balance. Psychological imbalance has a bad influence on the palm pattern, whereas improving coordination of mind and body improves it. To institute a program of improving the palm pattern of children of primary-school age or over, it is important first to carry out the test explained below.

Have paper and pencil ready and blindfold the child. Then have the child draw ten parallel lines about ten centimeters long each (FIG. 176). Neither the palm nor the fingers of the drawing hand nor those of the idle hand should touch the table top. Right-handed people should draw with their right hands, and left-handed ones with their left. Examine the finished drawings in the light of the following explanations.

Fig. 176   Judging the condition of the mind from hand-drawn parallel lines

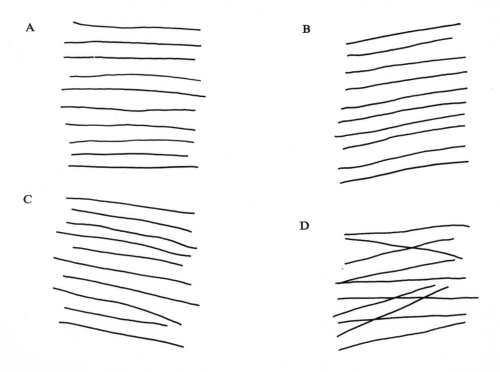

A

B

C

D

A. A child who draws parallel lines like these is psychologically stable, and his palm pattern is already developing in a good way.

B. A child who draws lines that all rise to the right tends to be extroverted and bright-natured but to lack powers of concentration. His palm pattern may be improved by training him in perseverance and the willingness to see things through to their conclusions.

C. A child who draws lines that all descend to the right is extremely nervous and introverted. His palm pattern can deteriorate because of his tendency to lack self-confidence and to think negatively.

D. Lines overlapping in places like these indicate irritability and lack of sleep and may be forewarnings of some disorders. When they appear, it is probably a good idea to have a physical examination or have x-rays taken.

On the basis of my own experience, using the work of the Brazillian psychologist F. W. Miller as reference, I evolved this test and have been using it since 1960. As the following examples show, once the psychological causes have been ascertained through this test, it is possible to apply various therapeutic methods.

1. Zen-like psychological training

Often Zen-like disciplines are effectively used in training children. Zen training can dramatically alter the pattern of the palm, which, in great priests, is often very different from the pattern with which they were born. For instance, it sometimes happens that, as in FIG. 177, a priest whose palm is pattern like (A) at birth, develops a pattern like (B) in the thirties; that is, the Intellect and Emotion Lines have coalesced in something like the *masukake* pattern. Yoga and other specialized physical training regimens too have an effect similar to that produced by Zen.

Fig. 177   Changing the pattern through special training

A

B

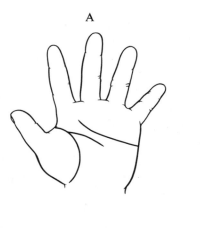
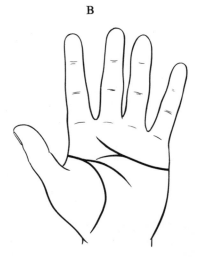

This ability of Zen and Yoga to change the palm pattern is related to the effect occupation has. The patterns of karate specialists and kick-boxers change because of their work. The thumbs of practitioners of shiatsu thicken; and their Life Lines become clear, as the hand of noted shiatsu specialist Tokujirō Namikoshi reveals. For similar reasons, the hands of people whose work is largely physical have simple patterns with clear, deep basic lines but few small lines, whereas people whose work involves psychological stress have many fine creases and lines in their palms. The same contrast can be observed in the simple, clear palm patterns of strong, hale, and hearty children and children who tend to be nervous and sensitive.

2. *Hypnotic suggestion*
Some primary- and middle-school teachers are trained in hypnosis and can use it in different ways with their children. Ideally, however, this method should be employed under the supervision of a specialist.

3. *Using palmistry as guidance in autosuggestion*
Because they enjoy it, primary- and middle-school children can easily be trained to make judgments on the basis of palmistry. Though hypnosis requires specialist assistance, this autosuggestion method employing the palm pattern can be employed by anyone. I once had excellent results from using it with a fifth-grade primary-school boy who, congenitally of weak constitution, aggravated the risk of catching frequent colds because he ignored his parents' and teachers' repeated instructions to gargle well after going out of doors.

Once I said to the boy, "Let's compare our palms." Then I pointed out to him the chainlike creases on his Life Line and showed him that my palm was free of them. I explained that individuals with such creases are often born with weak throats and can become seriously ill if they fail to gargle. Thereafter, this child, who had formerly been completely recalcitrant on the subject, never failed to gargle after coming home from school or going out.

The Case of a Mentally Retarded Child

The case of a congenitally mentally retarded child, whose palm pattern was like one of the three shown in FIG. 178 shows how psychological training can alter an unfortunate situation for the better.

The palm patterns of mentally retarded children are by no means identical. The one in (B) is that of Kiyoshi Yamashita, a painter of such stature as to be referred to as the Vincent van Gogh of Japan. Yamashita was mentally retarded but was fortunate enough to encounter Dr. Ryūzaburō Shikiba, who had devoted his life to helping such children and who recognized the boy's artistic ability, cultivated him, helped him to success, and thus saved him from the fate of ordinary children in his plight. In these days, when much effort is going into research and guidance for the sake of rehabilitating retarded children and the victims of

Fig. 178   Palm patterns indicating mental retardation

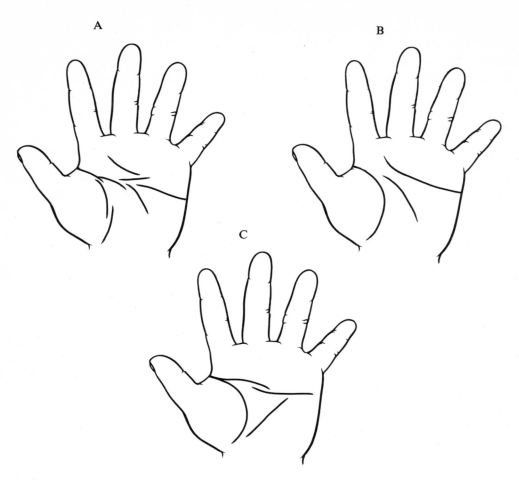

cerebral paralysis, it seems likely that children with this palm pattern too can be helped to find their own way in society.

Yamashita's palm pattern, which is different from the ordinary, was of the C Type, indicating artistic sensitivity and imagination. After Yamashita mastered the collage technique of making pictures, the configurations of his Intellect and Emotion Lines altered. In other words, it is possible to alter the palm patterns of even mentally retarded individuals through training, thus increasing the likelihood of their manifesting their talents to a fuller extent.

Psychologists divide retarded children into three categories: idiots, who have an Intelligence Quota (IQ) of less than twenty, are incapable of expressing themselves verbally, and have difficulty standing alone; imbeciles, who have an IQ of between twenty and fifty; and morons, who have an IQ of between fifty and seventy-five. Retarded people with the (B) hand pattern, who are often capable of artistic work if they are properly guided, are usually of the moron type.

Those with the (A) hand pattern are often idiots, whose education requires the greatest effort and patience, although sometimes repeated instruction in simple manual operations can alter the palm pattern. The palm pattern, with many irregular creases, of people of the (C) type can best be altered through work involving the motion of the entire body and of the fingers. Put into the right environment, with the help of a good teacher, these people can put their abilities to use in a new life that employs the best of which they are capable.

Physical Training to Alter the Palm Pattern

I have already discussed the important connections between the operations of the thumb and the development of the Life Line, the operations of the index and middle fingers and the development of the Intellect Line, and the motions of the little and ring fingers in the development of the Emotion Line.

Different parts of the hand come into play in the three basic manual operations. In gripping large ball-like or polelike objects, when strength is needed, the thumb is very important. This kind of motion demands what is called grasp-power gripping. In more delicate motions, like withdrawing a pin or using a screwdriver, however, the index and middle fingers play a major role. This kind of work requires precision gripping. In other words, the thumb is of major importance when the power of the whole hand is needed, and the index and middle fingers are vital to partial use of the hand. The little and ring fingers are important in touching things and making tactile judgments of their size.

In infants, these three functions develop gradually. For instance, an infant of about two months grasps building blocks by wrapping the entire hand around them. At three months, the infant grasps the object between the thumb and the four fingers in what can be called a grasp. At this age, light gripping with the fingertips is still impossible. At four months, the child is able to hold things in a pincerlike grip using the thumb and index finger.

The American child-psychologist A. Davis says that environment and individual differences influence the development of the hands' ability to function in these ways. For instance, the development is retarded in newborn infants who live in isolated places or who are brought up in orphanages in underprivileged countries.

Training to enable an infant to perform these three functions smoothly is effective in improving his palm pattern. First training should deal with smooth movement of the thumbs and then with hand movement centered on the thumb, index, and middle fingers. And these exercises should be combined with such others as opening and closing the little and ring fingers. In addition to improving the hand pattern, this regimen has a salutary effect on the child's intellectual development.

1)   To improve the Life Line, repeated gripping of the hand and extension and bending of the thumb simultaneously with both hands are effective.

2)   To improve the Intellect Line, have the child pick up small things like grains of rice from the top of a table, one by one, and put them in a bowl on an average of fifty times a day. This makes use of the connection between the thumb and index finger and the brain.

3) To improve the Emotion Line, repeated opening and closing of the tensed little and ring fingers are effective, as is bending the middle and ring fingers only while holding the little and index fingers and the thumb extended. Movements to improve the palm pattern by fostering manual dexterity at an early age should be taken into consideration in the selection of toys for children. In recent years, cerebral physiologists have come to believe that manual dexterity has an improving effect on the cerebrum.

> For children of ages two to three—Building blocks improve the Intellect Line; and balls, crayons, and dolls improve the Emotion Line.
> For children of ages three to five—Building blocks improve the Life and Intellect Lines. Paper dolls and dolls that can be dressed and undressed improve the Intellect Line. Modeling clay improves the total palm pattern.

In the preceding pages, I have discussed the human hand from such various angles as manifestations of personality, illness, and fate. The science of palmistry and the knowledge it has amassed are widely applied and put to use in scholarship today. I have carried out my own research for over thirty years, and the more I study the more enthusiastic I become. The many puzzles remaining unsolved in connection with it probably arise more from the mysteries of human beings themselves than from the hand as such.

The number of physicians and anthropologists demonstrating an interest in the hand is growing. But much of their research is nonsensical when viewed from the standpoint of old-fashioned, orthodox scholarship. The mysteries of the hand cannot be plumbed through traditionally accepted methods like systematization and rationalization but demand a totally new field of learning—humanistic psychology. Just as the Renaissance brought on a revamping of human values, so the twenty-first century is expected by many to produce a radically novel science of humanity. If so, this new kind of study may give us the wisdom to see humanity more accurately and thus may elucidate the persisting mysterious aspects of palmistry.

Appendix

Palm Patterns of World Celebrities

De Gaulle, Charles André Marie Joseph (1890–1970)

Characteristics: As is shown in the figure, the right hand is of the AH III Type, while the left is of the BH III Type. The Life Line is double, and the Fate Line is single and clear.

An extremely emotional person who becomes intoxicated with his own words.
The figure is based on a photograph of President De Gaulle's hands published in a book entitled *Le Passé et l'Avenir par les Lignes de la Main* in 1956. As is typical in active people, the thumb is very long and strongly made. A long Fate Line like the one in his hand occurs frequently in the palms of politicians. The most interest-

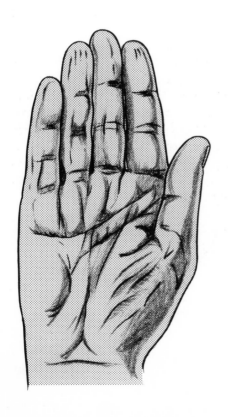

ing aspect of De Gaulle's palm is the way the Emotion Line is broken and bent (in the outer area), clearly revealing a volatile personality and the trait of being carried away easily with one's own words. The classical AH III Type of palm occurs often in intelligent military men and politicians. Unlike politicians with vague Fate Lines, who frequently encounter trouble and lack chances to manifest their powers to the full, those with palm patterns like De Gaulle's usually enjoy wide popular support and stay in power for a long time. But the vagueness visible in the upper part of his Fate Line (which indicates the late years of life) clearly reveals the tragic loss he suffered in 1969.

Einstein, Albert (1879–1955)

Characteristics: The Intellect Line (C-Type) begins from a point extended from between the middle and index fingers (on a broken-line extension). The palm print of the hypothenar manifests a whorl.

Symbol of abundant ideas

Albert Einstein's palm patterns were made public in a book by the English palmist Noël Jaquin. The world famous theoretical physicist and winner of the Nobel prize for physics in 1921 was deeply interested in palmistry, which he said could develop into a new kind of study of life in the future (Noël Jaquin, *Secrets of Hand-Reading*).

The pattern is a variant of the CH I Type, having an extremely long Intellect Line with islandlike creases on it. Many creases line the palm, especially on the side of the hypothenar, which is characterized by a whorl pattern. Usually the pattern in this region (which resembles fingerprints) is of a flowing type. The whorl appears here often in people who make special discoveries or develop ideas around which to formulate a whole field of study. For instance, H. H. Wilder, the world authority on the study of fingerprints, had a pattern of this same kind.

Often people with such a pattern are highly imaginative and come up with ideas and discoveries inconceivable to ordinary human beings. A splitting into two lines of the end of the Intellect Line, like that seen in Einstein's palm, occurs in people in whom theorizing powers and creative intuition are well balanced.

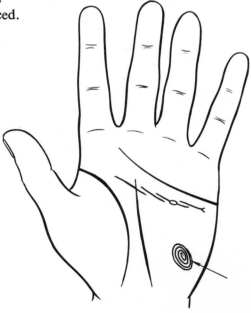

Mann, Thomas (1875–1955)

Characteristics: The Intellect Line is extremely long. Its terminal point and that of the Fate Line extend to the hypothenar (the Mount of the Moon).

A feminine hand type

The palm pattern of novelist and Nobel-prize winner Thomas Mann is feminine in that the hand is small and the palm marked with many fine creases. Men engaged in artistic and creative work frequently have basically feminine hands like this. When the hand is divided into right and left halves by the line at the middle finger, the hypothenar side has more creases than the opposite one.

Psychologist and researcher in the field of the human hand Charlotte Wolff calls the hypothenar side of this hand the unconscious zone and says it is well developed and covered with many creases in people who are highly sensitive and talented. In contrast to it, the thumb side of the hand is better developed in people who do conscious work and are intensely self-conscious. In people who have a powerful desire to be conspicuous, the bases of the index finger and the thumb are well fleshed and covered with many creases. The knuckles of the hands of very sensitive people are prominent and of the so-called double type. Such knuckles could be seen in the hands of Aldous Huxley and Jean Cocteau as well as in those of Thomas Mann. The topmost joint of the finger is sometimes enlarged into what are called philosophical knots, which indicate a fondness for philosophical thought.

Gide, André (1869–1951)

This is an E-Type hand in which the Life Line cuts well inside the Intellect Line. There are many creases on the Mount of the Moon. People with this kind of hand tend to be imaginative and creative but to be delicate and very introverted. The hand is more feminine than masculine. The semicircular crease known as the Girdle of Venus appears at the base of the middle and ring fingers.

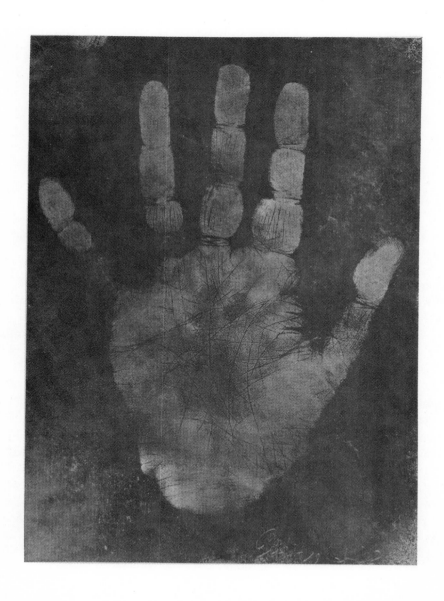

Montherlant, Henry de (1896–1972)

In the palm of this active and aggressive writer, the Life and Intellect Lines are separated in the B-Type pattern.

Cocteau, Jean (1889–1963)

With a clear Girdle of Venus at the base of the middle and ring fingers, the palm pattern of this famous French writer can be called that of a person with great aesthetic and artistic sensitivity. Because the Intellect Line is straight, the pattern is, not L, but H. This indicates a person with exceptionally keen powers of theorizing and analytical thought.

Miller, Henry (1891–1980)

Characteristics: Slightly different version of the F-Type hand. The three basic lines all converge in one place, and there is a clear semicircular crease at the base of the middle finger.

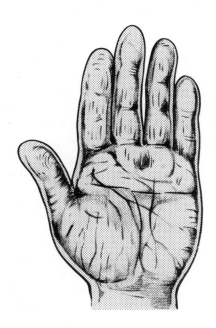

Abnormal interest in sex

The hand pattern of this American author of such bold books as *Sexus* and *Nexus* is, as might be expected, extraordinary and indicates a personality incapable of being satisfied with the usual constantly in search of something different. The long semicircular crease at the base of the middle finger indicates an abnormal interest in sex.

Other characteristics of the hand are the pattern at the base of the middle finger and the Line of Apollo extending vertically from the ring finger. These traits indicate keen sensitivity and artistic creativity. Long vertical lines usually mean talent in literature and other kinds of expressive work. Japanese authors too whose writing is highly distinctive have hand patterns similar to Miller's.

The considerable length of the tip of the thumb indicates great self-confidence. Such people tend to be stubborn and not to change their minds once they have made them up. Furthermore, the shape of the thumb is deeply connected with masculinity. People in whom it is long and well fleshed tend to have great vitality and sexual vigor. Famous French author and avant-garde motion-picture director Jean Cocteau had thumbs shaped very much like these.

Roosevelt, Anna Eleanor (1884–1962)—*Wife of Franklin Delano Roosevelt, thirty-second president*

Characteristics: A very unusual hand for a woman. The Fate Line extends from the wrist in a straight line to the middle finger. There are many triangular creases on the palm.

Exceptional ability to observe the future

One of the most noted of all American first ladies, Eleanor Roosevelt was active in many fields and a great psychological support for her husband from the time when he was stricken with infantile paralysis. Often women, in whom it is rare, with this kind of hand pattern, with a perfectly straight Fate Line, are stronger and more active than men and chafe under the restrictions frequently imposed on the female sex. They have powers of decisiveness, can make full use of their abilities in the circumstances in which they find themselves, and are keen observers of the future.

Triangular configurations too characterize Eleanor Roosevelt's palm. The Intellect Line, the Life Line, and the crease of the hypothenar form a large triangle as do the Intellect Line, the Fate Line, and the crease of the hypothenar and the Intellect Line, the Fate Line, and the crease of the hypothenar. In addi-

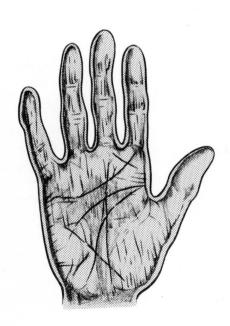

tion, there are small triangular creases at the base of the index finger. Palmistry interprets these triangular creases as signs of great happiness. The triangular crease at the base of the index finger indicates leadership ability and the charm to guide people.

The large triangle formed by the three basic lines indicates ability to put complex problems in order and to work in a brisk and efficient manner. It is often found in company vice-presidents and in people with ability as advisers.

Sukarno, Devi—*Wife of the late President Sukarno of Indonesia*

Characteristics: Intellect Line begins well below the Life Line, the terminal part of which is split in two. The Marriage Line is long and intertwines with vertical crease at the base of the ring finger.

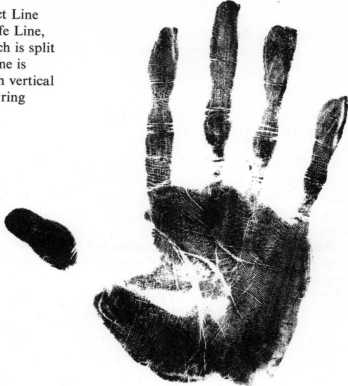

Persevering and ambitious person

The palm pattern of this celebrity, who was the third wife of president Sukarno of Indonesia and later caused a stir in the mass media over her relation with a noted Japanese motion-picture actor, is of the EL II Type, which is frequent in beautiful women.

The interesting aspect of the palm is the way the Marriage Line at the base of the little finger mingles with creases at the base of the ring finger. From the distant past, this unusual characteristic has been interpreted as indicating the advent of a Prince Charming. The longer this line, the greater the person's power to captivate the opposite sex. The split terminal section of the Life Line indicates living abroad when it becomes impossible to live in the place of one's birth. The origin of the Intellect Line well below the Life Line is a symbol of ambition. People with palms like this are frequently misunderstood by those around them but persevere and refuse to demonstrate psychological insecurity.

Women in whom the Intellect Line begins well below the Life Line tend to be sexually passionate and to like passive love; men who have had affairs with them find them unforgettable.

The smaller a woman's hands, the greater her sexual ardor. Women with large hands or large thumbs have little sexual appeal.

Bernhardt, Sarah

Women in whom the beginnings of Intellect and Life Lines are widely separated, as they are in the hand of this famous French actress, are often highly active, adventurous, and outstanding. Such a pattern occurs in many of the popular entertainers of today. For example, the palm pattern of Elizabeth Taylor is similar to this one. The long Line of Apollo and Fate Line are typical of people showing greater devotion to work than to home life.

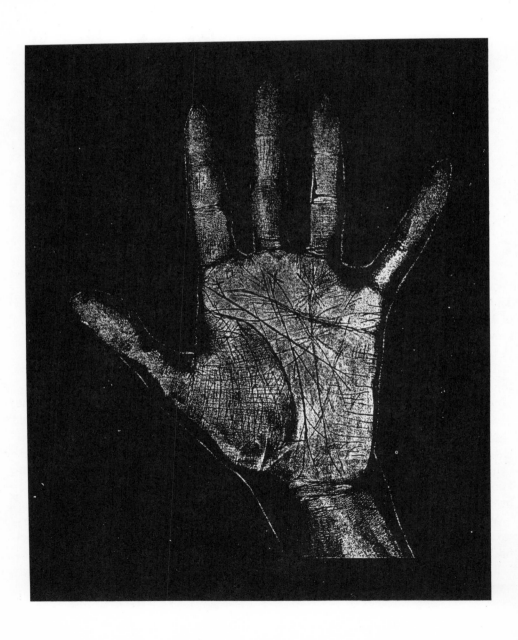

Morita, Akio (1921—)—*Founder of the Sony Corporation*

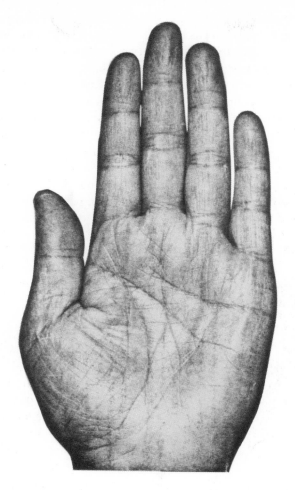

General: The hand is slender, feminine, and elegant in appearance and reveals a personality with aesthetic sensitivity and outstanding creativity. People with such hands are thinkers who are warm, bold, and sometimes nervous. Charlotte Wolff has said that this kind of hand occurs frequently among members of famous European aristocratic families. They are delicate, dislike quarreling, and sometimes prefer to be alone. Their instincts are excellent, and they always take the future into consideration before acting. They are gentle and generous.

Individual analysis: The Fate Line is long and clear, extending from the wrist straight toward the middle finger. This case indicates how the Fate Line is the barometer of success in the hands of businessman. The longer the line, the greater the individual's chance of acquiring great power. The famous Japanese military ruler Toyotomi Hideyoshi (1536–98) is said to have had a Fate Line extending halfway up the middle finger. A close examination reveals a second Fate Line that turns outward indicating success with the help of others. The first Fate Line indicates success as an outcome of one's own efforts. In other words, this pattern is that of a person who can seize the chances offered him because he is supported by two kinds of fate. The two lines cross at a point that suggests a sudden change of fate at the age of about twenty-seven or twenty-eight.

The Intellect Line extends straight upward in a curve so regular that it might have been drawn with a compass. This kind of line indicates a clever mind with keen powers of analytical thought. The upward curve often occurs in people with a strong attachment to money plus the ability to acquire it and make it multiply.

The Emotion Line is split in two and moves in the direction of the base of the index finger. This kind of line occurs in people who are very reluctant to reveal their own emotions. When they take a physiological dislike to someone, even though they may intellectually understand that person's ideas, they find it impossible to sympathize with them. The two semicircular creases at the base of the middle finger are called the Girdle of Venus and indicate aesthetic sense and an interest in dressing well.

Along the Line of Apollo, which indicates success in business and money matters, occurs a triangular crease, which occurs with great rarity and means immense and unexpected financial aggrandizement.

Honda, Sōichirō (1906—)—*Founder of Honda Motors*

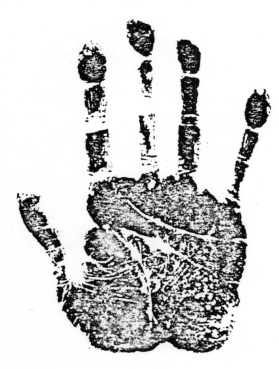

The three basic lines are clear, and the Intellect Line is straight in this H-Type palm pattern. The Type-III Emotion Line suggests an optimistic person who does not worry about minor theoretical matters in making decisions. The hand is characterized by a long, thick thumb, suggesting a vigorous person with strong will-power and the perseverance to overcome difficulties and hardships.

Yi, Byeong Cheol (1910—)—
Chairman of the Samsung Group

Characteristics: A single, clear, long Fate Line marks the palm; and the Emotion Line extends to the base of the index finger.

The pattern of a person blessed in economic fortune
Kōnosuke Matsushita, founder of the National Electrical Company, is one of the most famous self-made men in Japan. Byeong Cheol Yi, founder of the Samsung Group, which is now one of the biggest financial groups in Asia, is referred to as the Kōnosuke Matsushita of Korea. His palm pattern is of the AH III Type, which occurs often in Japanese business leaders. Yi made the vast fortune between his twenties and forties. His palm reveals the long Fate Line and the Line of Apollo that occur frequently in people whose economic fortunes are strong.

Matsushita, Kōnosuke (1894—)

The foremost businessman in Japan
The palm pattern is characterized by a clear Fate Line and Line of Apollo and by a vertical line leading from the base of the little finger. All three converge at one place. For many years this has been considered the palm pattern of millionaires and people who are blessed with good fortune in work and financial affairs. The Fate Line and the Life Line overlap and rise, indicating a person who has exerted effort to attain his present position.

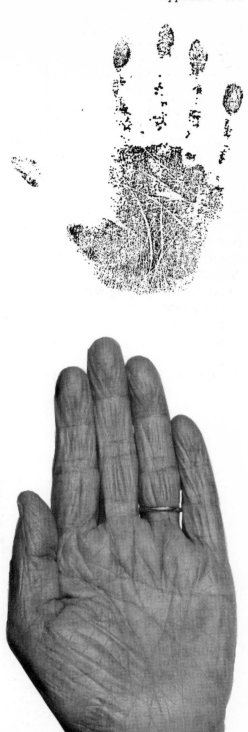

Changes in Palm Patterns

Changes occurring with age

FIGS. A, B, and C reveal the changes that took place in the palm pattern of one person from infancy into adulthood.

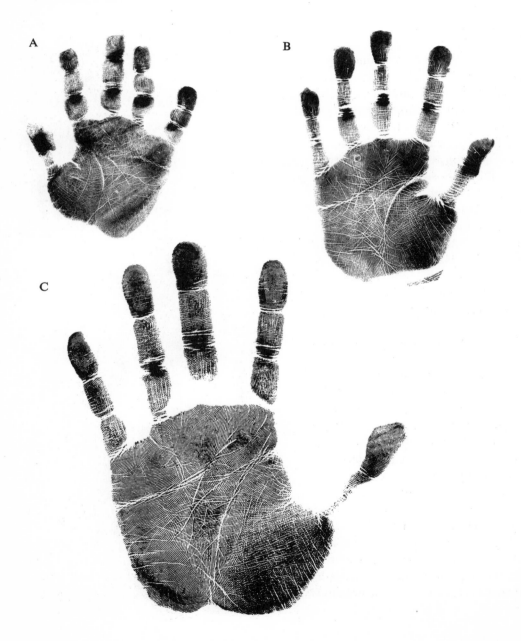

Broken palm patten as a sign of illness and sudden death

This broken palm pattern (FIG. A) occurred in the hand of Japanese champion sumo wrestler Tama-no-umi and represents a severance of the Life Line. Though he was confident in his own stamina, an operation for appendicitis caused his sudden death. And this pattern occurred in his palm immediately prior to the surgery. Three years earlier, the Life Line had been continuous and unbroken (FIG. B). The break appeared just before his fatal operation.

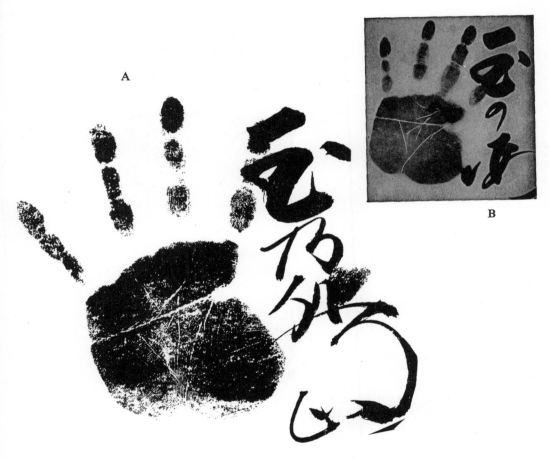

A

B

Palm pattern of a person killed in an accident

This is the palm pattern of the Japanese singer Kyū Sakamoto (1941–85), famous all over the world for his hit song *Sukiyaki*, who was killed in the crash of a Japan Airlines jet in August, 1985, the worst air accident in history. A comparison between the pattern as it had been earlier and as it was a year before the accident reveals a change in the Fate Line. In addition, there is a cross-shaped configuration on the Life Line. Though connection between palm pattern and illness have been recognized, the reason why the pattern should change at about the time of an accident is unknown.

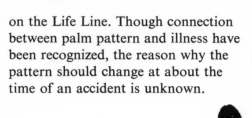

Traffic Accident—Sada, Keiji

In the palm pattern as it was a few months before this man died in a traffic accident, square configurations had appeared on the Life Line and islandlike irregularities on the Intellect Line.

Bibliography

Aussoleil, G. *La Main Reflet de Votre Caractère*. Paris: Retz, 1982.

Berges, J. *Les Gestes et la Personalité*. Hachette, 1967.

Berry, T. J. *The Hand as a Mirror of Systemic Disease*. F. Davis, 1963.

Blechsmidt, E. *The Stages of Human Development before Birth*. London: W. B. Saunders, 1961.

Blin, C. *Votre Main*. Rocher, 1980.

Brun, J. *La Main et l'Esprit*. P.U.F., 1968.

Bunnel, S. *Surgery of the Hand*. J. B. Lippincott, 1956.

Cheiro. *Cheiro's Language of the Hand*. Wyman & Sons, 1958.

Cummins, H., and C. Midlo. *Fingerprints, Palms and Soles*. Blakiston, 1943.

Darwin, C. *Expression of Emotion in Man and Animal*. London: Watts, 1943.

Gettings, F. *The Book of the Hand*. Paul Hamlyn, 1965.

Hutchinson, B. *La Main Reflet du Destin*. Deux Coq d'Or, 1969.

————. *The Handbook on Hands Awareness*. Surridges, 1978.

Jacques, d'Iseneure. *Le Passé et l'Avenir par les Lignes de la Main*. Paris: Guy le Prat, 1956.

Jacquin, Noël. *The Hand Speaks*.

Jones, F. Wood. *The Principles of Anatomy as Seen in the Hand*. London: Churchill, 1920.

Korman, B. *Hands—the Power of Hand Awareness*. Surridges, 1978.

Mangin, H. *Abrégé de Chiroscopie Medical*. Dangles, 1951.

Morant, G. *Traité de Chiromancie Chinoise*. Guy Trédaniel, 1978.

Peruchio, S. *Chiromancie*. Pierre l'Amy, 1697.

Sen, K. C. *Hast Samudrika Shastra*. Bombay: D. B. Tarapo Revaia, 1969.

Siler, A. *Chiromancie Royale et Nouvelle*. Daniel Gayet, 1697.

Sorell, W. *The Story of the Human Hand*. London: Weidenfeld, 1968.

Spier, J. *The Hands of Children*. Sager Publications, 1944.

Vaschide, N. *Essai sur la Psychologie de la Main*.

Weber, F. *Votre Caractère*. F. Médicis, 1954.

Weissbrodt, Raymond. *Les Lignes de Votre Main Parlent*. Paris: Tchou, 1982.

Wolff, Charlotte. *La Main Humaine*. P.U.F., 1952.

————. *The Hand in Psychological Diagnosis*. Methuen, 1951.

————. *Psychology of Gesture*. Methuen, 1948.

List of Figures

Index